MONSTERS IN MY HOUSE

A TRUE STORY

WALT MCKINLEY

Paperback ISBN: 978-0-578-35860-4

This book is dedicated to everyone who has ever experienced trauma. I hope this memoir gives you inspiration, strength, and tools to propel your healing journey and unlock life's abundance. I want you to know that you are not alone, you are not broken, and you do not need to be fixed. You are powerful, you are a warrior, you are a fighter, and you are extraordinary. Whether you're taking your first step, in the middle, or have done the healing work in your journey, I am proud of you for choosing to step through the pain and into the happiness you deserve.

To my wife, Stephanie, you are the most amazing human being I've ever known. I'm blessed God gifted you to me. You've loved me through my brokenness and empowered me to be the person I am today. Your love, compassion, selflessness, support, and, most of all, patience are the reasons our love has stood the test of time. You are my rock and my everything. I love you!

To my daughters, Monica and Brianna, you completed my humanity. You bring me more joy than I ever dreamed and I couldn't imagine life without you. Having the honor of being your dad is everything I wished it would be, and life's greatest reward. I love you!

To Aunt Dianna, you were the light in my darkness when I didn't think I could hang on any longer. Against all odds, you had the courage to rescue a broken teenager and breathed life back into my soul. I will be forever grateful for the impact you've had on me and how your love has changed our family legacy forever. I love you!

"Your History Does Not Define Your Destiny"

– T.D. Jakes

TABLE OF CONTENTS

Prologue: Terrified of the Dark (circa 1984)   1

Chapter 1: A Broken System   9

Chapter 2: Wild and Free   16

Chapter 3: First Day of School   36

Chapter 4: Kidnapped   47

Chapter 5: A New Addition   56

Chapter 6: Dumped on the Sidewalk   67

Chapter 7: Locked In The Basement   78

Chapter 8: Ocean Beach   100

Chapter 9: The Darkness Returns   115

Chapter 10: Running From Prosecution   138

Chapter 11: Justice   161

Chapter 12: Finding My Voice   189

Chapter 13: Adulthood   214

Chapter 14: The Navy   236

Chapter 15: Submarines   255

Chapter 16: Setbacks and Comebacks   269

Chapter 17: The Miracle of Life   280

Chapter 18: Keys to Living an Extraordinary Life   303

Acknowledgements   315

About the Author   317

PROLOGUE
TERRIFIED OF THE DARK (CIRCA 1984)

I sat alone crying and screaming, the darkness enveloping me like a cold, damp blanket as shivers of fear moved up my spine. My heartbeat pulsed into my head and sweat dripped down my entire body. Just moments ago, GI Joe was fighting for freedom against Cobra Command in the headquarters at Walt's world (a.k.a., my room). The plastic, muscular arms of GI Joe's first sergeant, Duke, who serve as the purveyor of freedom, tangled against Cobra Commander, the evil villain who was willing to do harm to anyone weaker. They were locked in intense combat. Duke and the other Joes heard the call for help from the little, green army men who didn't have the strength to fight against Cobra Commander and the Dreadnoks.

During the fight, one of the Dreadnoks must have been blown up and thrown into the living room or maybe stuck on the way to the battle. Either way, leaving my toy in the living room proved disastrous. This was the worst-case scenario because, at eight years old, I should have been responsible enough to keep my toys picked up. There were consequences if I didn't. Heavy ones.

Soon, I heard him yell out, "I told that stupid ass to keep his fucking toys out of here!"

Then I heard the familiar, heavy footsteps of his steel-toed boots coming down the hall. The stomping they made immediately threw my body into fight or flight mode. There were exactly ten steps to my room. These steps warned me and gave my mind, body, and soul time to prepare for the inevitable beating. My heart pounded as my real-life Cobra Commander, my stepdad Bruce, came to my room.

One, two, three, four…

My mind raced in terror. I prayed that Duke was here to protect me. After all, if he could save the world he could save me, right? I picked up Duke and looked at his fit physique, gun, and the strength in his eyes. Courage incarnate. Where was Duke when I need him?

Five, six, seven, eight…

The steps grew closer, and my terror grew. I lifted my head and looked at the door in terrified anticipation.

Nine, ten!

The intensity of the fear and the feeling of doom made the last two steps seem to last forever.

Bam!

The door slammed open and bounced off the door spring at the bottom, causing the familiar *boing* sound at impact. I looked up to see the Dreadnok flying towards my head.

My stepdad screamed, "I told you I didn't want to see any fucking toys in the living room. Ever!"

My reflexes kicked in like a cat; I jumped up as I watched the Dreadnok action figure sail toward me at slow motion. Or it seemed like slow motion. I turned just fast enough to dodge the inbound missile. It flew past me in a blur, coming close enough I could hear the whistle of the wind in my ear. I turned back, and his hand struck my face, making my ears ring with a piercing buzz. The impact left me dizzy and floundering off balance. I fell on one knee. But soon I was brought to my feet. He yanked me up by the neck like a Boa constrictor.

My stepdad grabbed my hair and yanked my head back. "Your ass is mine!" he yelled.

His hands were callused from construction work and seemed to cover my entire head with every smack. My knees felt like those of a baby deer struggling to propel itself forward. My eyesight blurred as tears streamed down my face.

I knew what was coming and I was terrified. I pleaded for him to let me go and professed extreme regret. "I'm sorry. I'll pick up my toys better next time. Please don't. I'm sorry. Please!"

The begging became a litany that couldn't sway him. My voice faded away, falling on deaf ears and a black heart. I knew then what was coming next. I pled for my life. I knew a monster was waiting for me where I was about be taken.

I searched for my mother as he pulled me by my hair through the house. I hoped she could be my Duke—my hero—in that moment. *There she is*, I thought as my heart tried to leap out of my body. Even as young as I was, I kept praying she'd help me. I was wrong.

My mother only stared back at me with her crystal blue eyes, her eyebrows lifted just slightly, her mouth not saying a word. There was pain on her face, sympathy for me. But she was too scared and too numb to stop things.

Bruce ripped the door of the basement open, and the damp musty smell of concrete and stagnant air filled my nose. The cold air of the winter in Indiana whooshed up like a tornado and gave me chills. He yanked on my hair, attempting to throw me into the basement. I resisted with every ounce of energy I could muster. I didn't want to be thrown into the dungeon where the monster lived.

I heard the monster from the top of the stairs heavily breathing, laughing, saying in a low grumbling voice, "Come here, it's only you and me again. I hope you're ready!"

Bruce grabbed me by the back of the neck and forced me into the basement. He pushed me back. I fell to the third step and turned to see his face, his teeth bared and his hatred stifling. Time seemed to stand still as he slammed the door shut. The sound reverberated through my soul and left me paralyzed. I had to choose between two monsters. I ran to the top step. But the lock clicked shut. I was trapped and filled with despair.

I sat on the top step and tried to let my eyes adjust to the darkness. The panic began to overtake me. I screamed and hit the door.

"Please let me out! Please let me out! Please let me out!" I said over and over, wondering why this was happening to me.

I screamed louder and more frantically, like someone who had been buried alive. My body was in flight mode, but with no place to run. Then the door swung open and an immediate momentary feeling of relief came over me. For once, Bruce was going to show grace and let me out.

Thank you, thank God, thank my mom, and thank Duke.

I didn't care; I was willing to do anything and thank anyone who helped me escape. The feeling of elation was quickly replaced by the grim realization that my punishment was just beginning. "You want something to cry about, motherfucker?"

Bruce raised his hand. I flinched and backed up to the third step again. "Get to the bottom of the stairs. Now!" The seven remaining steps to the bottom seemed to take an eternity to complete; one by one, I made my way down the unfinished wooden steps, each one creaking under my tiny body. Standing at the bottom I thought, *Why can't I be courageous like Duke?*

Bruce stood at the top of the steps, his silhouette dark as the light from the kitchen hit his back and cast his shadow towards me. He slowly lifted up his arm and started laughing. I could tell exactly what he was holding, and I almost passed out from the fear. It was the monster, the mask he usually stored down here and used to torment me. Bruce knew I was terrified of it and took every opportunity to use it. He lifted the mask high into the air so I'd see it clearly and laughed. It was an evil laugh, one that pierced my heart.

His arm cocked behind his body as he threw the mask towards me. "Now you have something to cry about!"

The mask immediately took life in my imagination. I heard its feet rumbling down the steps like a wild herd of stampeding buffalo, getting closer and louder with every millisecond.

The mask hit my leg and I felt it tear into my flesh, claiming a chunk out of my shin. "I told you I would get you."

My imagination and fear ran wild.

The monster was a werewolf. Its skin was a battered and weathered white. It had bright white teeth except for the blood trickling down them, and it had a giant wild mane of neon green hair. It was the most evil and terrifying thing I had ever seen. The mask was a type of scary that made your heart palpitate just by seeing it in a corner. I let out a blood curdling scream of fear, kicking the mask off the small three-by-three concrete platform and down the steps into the main area of the basement. I grabbed my leg and attempted to fend off visions of me dying and being eaten alive by the werewolf.

I sat on the concrete floor and pulled myself into a ball, my back feeling the cold of the damp bricks and my eyes just peering over my crossed arms. Hugging my knees, I rocked back and forth as I screamed and cried. Not knowing if I would be down there for an hour, a day, or even if I would be alive when the door was opened weighed heavily on my sanity.

I heard the taps of nails on concrete as the monster paced in my imagination. Its heavy grunts came as it breathed, and the subtle whispers of *You're mine* all continued just as time seemed to stop.

The minutes turned into hours. I'd stopped screaming but my soul was still wounded. I sobbed softly to myself. Not those loud ones, but the cries that happen when you are all alone, feeling like nobody would ever save you. It was moments like these that I knew God was protecting me. I didn't know it was God then but, as the hours passed, I felt serenity replace my terror. I felt a rush of peace and saw a glowing light. The cold, damp concrete immediately felt warmer. My tears dried up, and my hope returned. It felt like a warm blanket enveloping my entire being, like the strongest arms I had ever felt wrapping around me to let me know I was safe. That my heart and soul were safe, as well.

I didn't realize it then but, in that prison of a basement and my torment, God saved my soul. He gave my skinny, frail, eight-year-old body the strength of one hundred Dukes. The Heavenly Father gave me the strength to keep moving forward one step at time.

Eventually, I was let out of the basement. When I came out, I squinted at the brightness of the lamp. I was in the basement for ten hours. It was like being thrown to my demise in the early morning and then released from purgatory in the evening after dark fell. God changed me that day. I knew it and could feel the strength He gave me still coursing through my veins and to combat the voices in my head. The Lord gave me the strength I needed to endure eight more years of tortuous physical and emotional abuse, neglect, and suffering at the hands of every adult in my life.

This is my harrowing but victorious story of how I went through the depths of hell, was chased by the devil, and ultimately saved by the grace of God. Much hard work broke the cycle of abuse, creating a legacy of personal and professional success along the way. I'm not a survivor or victim of abuse; I am a *Warrior* of abuse and thriving!

CHAPTER 1
A BROKEN SYSTEM

My first real memory was of searing pain shooting through my body like a rocket. I was about three years old and in foster care with my sister, Faith.

Just a few weeks prior to this moment, Faith and I were taken from our mother, Carol, due to abuse from our stepfather, Bruce. We were placed in foster care for the first time in my life, but these foster parents had evil intent from the moment we set foot in their house. My foster parents seemed nice to us in front of the CPS case workers, but behind closed doors they were quick to hit, beat, and torture us.

The pain started at my fingertips and reverberated down the entirety of my little three-year-old body. I tried to get away from my foster mother. My hand was already dripping with bright red blood. Her grip tightened around my slippery wrist. I made a fist with all my might and pulled with every ounce of strength I could muster. But I couldn't manage to get away. She squeezed my wrist even harder and pried my fingers from the white knuckled fist they were in. She pulled my hand between her arm and side, pushing me behind her, so she could get leverage enough to rip my fist fully open and amplify the pain she was doling out.

I let out a huge, defeated sigh as I lost the battle. Her hands were too big and strong for me to counter any longer. Pleased with her efforts, she began forcing splinters—fragments of wood about a half-inch long, retrieved from an old two-by-four on the back porch— under my fingernails between the skin and the nailbed. She pressed harder against my hand as I screamed out in pain and tried to wriggle free.

All the nerves in my fingers burned intensely like I'd just been hit by a lightning bolt. Those splinters destroyed these nerves one by one. She maniacally yelled at me to stop moving. I tasted cigarettes and coffee from her breath just inches away, as if they were directly in my mouth. Her breathing became heavier as her frustration grew. Her eyes stared at me in delight as she transferred the pain she was feeling back into my fingers and soul, taking a piece of my humanity with every slowly inserted splinter.

I couldn't see her face, just the outline of a figure with eyes dark as night. She slammed me to the ground. My breath left my body as I hit the floor. She laid over the top of my arm to gain control and pushed another splinter into my finger. It was like a hot knife slicing through butter as it burned through my skin. I couldn't move. The intensity and panic became a fever pitch and so overwhelming that I started to lose consciousness.

I lifted my eyes and could see Faith chained to the bed, her ocean blue eyes full of tears and frustration as she cried out to me. I couldn't understand what she was saying, but I could see the despair in those same eyes. Her hands waved wildly towards my body like she was praying for them to stretch into the next room.

Faith is two years older than me. When we were kids, she always tried to be my protector and took beatings or verbal abuse for me when she could. Faith was the one constant in my life, the one person I knew I could count on then and for years to come.

But we were terribly weak and malnourished, just walking skeletons of skin and bones. These were the kind of bodies that only came from starvation.

After the splinters, I wanted to just lay there and go to sleep forever, to have the pain taken away. I wanted to feel God's mercy and be anywhere but where I was. I felt my body begin to go limp, and the pain grow numb as I started to pass in and out of consciousness.

I closed my eyes and quit struggling, undergoing an out-of-body experience until I was eventually forced to stand. My foster mother dealt a harsh slap across my face. My cheek stung like I'd just been attacked by a jelly fish. The smack hit me like a ton of bricks and left me feeling like my head would explode. I couldn't feel my face then. For just a moment, I forgot about the pain being inflicted on my fingertips and focused on my face and the ringing in my ears.

Everything seemed to move more slowly. I looked down. There was blood on my knee-high socks, the three green stripes held my attention as they grew stained.

My foster mother was not placated in the least. She screamed out in a frantic, shrill voice, "Wake the fuck up!"

I felt the sensation of blood drip from my fingertips as the metallic smell of copper filled my nose. My foster mother grabbed my neck and walked me back to the closet. She yelled at me to get back in then shoved me from behind and sent me tumbling over—face first—into the vacuum.

I felt my nose swell.

In the closet, the smell of cigarettes was heavy, like a stifling stagnant smell in the air that never circulated. Coats, a vacuum, and miscellaneous items made the fit tight. I only had a little space to sit down. It was dark and I was scared. At least, though, I was being left alone. I sat quietly so she wouldn't come back, even though inside I was screaming in pain.

I began to pull the splinters out of the fingernails in my left hand. The blood made each splinter slick and hard to grab. I tried to focus my attention in the dark and closed my eyes. With effort, the first splinter slid out of my finger, causing a euphoria as the pressure and pain alleviated. With each splinter's removal, new life was breathed into my broken soul.

———

A couple of days later, my grandmother, Flo, showed up from Arizona. My grandmother was a champion for her grandkids, fighting and willing to do whatever it took to protect them. She was an old-school Irish woman who was tough as nails with a protective and nurturing heart of gold.

She drove the six hours from her home in Arizona to us in California because she had a bad feeling that something was wrong; a pit in her stomach telling her she absolutely had to run to us. The state allowed her to see us, but they wouldn't allow her to take and raise us despite her repeated attempts to bring us back to Arizona.

Grandma recalled to me before she passed that she showed up to our foster home and tried to play it calm like she was in California for a vacation and wanted to stop by to see me and Faith. My grandmother was full of fire when she saw my nailbeds and my arms filled with black, blue, and yellow bruises. She glared at our foster mother, ready to punch her out at any given moment. But she knew she'd need the support of Child Protective Services and the police, so she refrained.

Instead, Grandma sent Pop-Pop to the payphone to call the police and stayed at the house. Her posture, body language, tone and the fiery intensity in her eyes shone bright like an inferno as she kept me and Faith enveloped in her protective coat of love and compassion. We just had to wait until justice was served.

The police showed up to our door. Multiple officers entered the house in succession, their dark blue uniforms fully pressed, tidy, and neat badges glimmering in the sunlight. They turned down their walkie-talkies that squawked with codes and noise nobody understood.

My grandmother told them that we were being abused and grabbed my hand to show them the bruises and lifted up my shirt to expose more on the rest of my body. Her eyes were full of pain for her grandkids.

The officers asked me what happened. To the best of my three-year-old abilities, I told them about the splinters and the beatings we took. They turned to our foster mother and asked for her version of the story. She immediately became defensive, stating my sister was secretly abusing me and putting the splinters under my fingernails, causing the bruising.

The police called CPS, which then decided we needed to be removed from the home. Because there were no witnesses to the abuse and no one could be 100% sure what happened, they chose to separate me and my sister, putting us in different foster homes until the investigation was complete.

Two ladies from CPS came into the house with large black trash bags and put our clothes in them. They told us we were going to be OK, and they were here to help. When they finished, Faith and I were taken to different vehicles by separate CPS workers.

Faith realized we weren't going to the same cars and began to scream. "Don't take my brother!"

She fought to get away from the CPS worker and run to me. I panicked because she was crying and screaming and tried to reach for her. Each worker grabbed us away just before we got within arm's reach. Our emotions were running high as we begged and pleaded to be kept together to no avail.

After being separated from Faith, I was placed with a new and extremely loving foster mother. She had blond curly hair, glasses, a soft caring way, and treated me like I was her son, all while attempting to mend the wounds I'd been given at such a young age.

I wasn't aware at the time but soon learned that my mom was working behind the scenes to regain her custodial rights and get us back. She attended classes and any requirements the state put forth.

I was about three and a half when my mom won custody of me and my sister back from the state, but it didn't mean things were going to be better. She was still with Bruce, whose abuse was the reason we were in foster care to begin with.

CHAPTER 2
WILD AND FREE

I'm superman and I can fly, I thought to myself as I ran with the speed of a world-class sprinter towards the box under the branch of a giant oak tree. My four-year-old body was full of energy and surging towards the lowest branch that seemed like it was 200 feet in the air. I was superman and there wasn't any kryptonite around to slow me down, so I was going for it. I felt the grass under my feet, cool and soft, the air outside a mid-summer warmth with a light breeze that dried each drop of sweat on my body while I bit my tongue in full concentration and focus. I tasted the salty sweat as I got closer to the box I'd placed just below the tree branch and picked up my pace as I got near, my focus on only one thing: grabbing the branch.

"Here it comes! This time I'm going to make it!" I said to myself.

I took a step, then another—*bang!* I shot off the ground and felt like I'd been catapulted forward from a cannon, jumping as high as I could off of the box. I thought I was actually flying, and it felt so freeing. My hands hooked onto the branch of the oak tree and held on for life as my legs swayed almost as high as my head; if I released my grip now, I'd do a full somersault.

The tree was huge, standing about 30 feet high, with a giant base and leaves bigger than my hands. It was a sanctuary where I felt safe, where I could feel like Superman. I lifted my legs up towards the branch and my bare feet became like another set of hands as I shimmied towards the base of the trunk where I could grab another branch and start my ascent. The oak tree had a distinct smell from the others; this sweetish earthy aroma filled my nose. The fissured deep grooves of the bark were rough on my skin, lightly scraping it with every movement. I grabbed for another branch and made sure I had a good grip this time, especially since I'd fallen at this point more than I could count.

I scampered up the tree with the precision only the flexibility and strength a young kid could muster and stood on a branch about 20 feet in the air. Triumphant, I felt the power of something so strong and giant that nothing could hurt it or me. The leaves sounded like a symphony in the wind with each dark green leaf swaying and whooshing a loud but peaceful song. I closed my eyes and imagined I was Superman or the giant oak tree—strong, resilient, and able to protect myself and Faith.

I felt free.

Faith called me in for lunch, I grabbed each branch on my way down like an Olympian gymnast. As my feet hit the ground, I looked up and puffed out my chest with a sense of awe and pride knowing that I could do anything.

I ran inside to eat, my stomach feeling hunger pains and my thirst unquenchable. I grabbed the package of Wonder Bread and Faith grabbed the bologna from our green refrigerator. I went to the counter and filled our plastic Tupperware cup with lukewarm water. I guzzled and gulped each drop of water like I'd just finished walking across the Sahara desert, breathing heavily as I finished the glass and came up for air. We slapped two pieces of bread together with the bologna and ran back outside to eat it. The doughy soft bread stuck to the roof of my mouth as I took a bite.

Outside was my safe space. I could run free, climb, explore, and do whatever I wanted without being in eyesight of Bruce. Being within range typically came with physical or emotional abuse. After seven moves in the first four years of my life, I finally felt like I had a permanent home, one where I wouldn't be bounced around between my mom, dad, and foster parents.

———

The music was loud as it came through the tower speakers stretched from the living room to the patio in our backyard. The Eagles' song "Take It Easy" played and all of the adults congregated together and sang it out loud. Empty and half-drunk Miller High Life beer cans were strewn all over the tables and ground, some with cigarette butts in them, some crushed or smashed, and even a small tower on the picnic table near the cooler. The smell of marijuana filled the air as the adults passed around the green grass, using a clip with a brown feather attached on the back to hold the end of the joints, making sure they didn't waste any of it. I saw them all coughing and giggling as they blew the smoke into the air, some of them even trying to inhale the cloud.

This was a common occurrence in our house. Many weekends we hosted parties from Friday through Sunday with many of the adults crashing out on the couch or lawn chairs until late in the morning. Alcohol, drugs, and about 10-15 kids ran around the giant yard with no adult supervision until late into the night. This was all the norm and tonight was no different.

I turned to see a group laughing in jubilation. Many of them hugged each other, arms draped around necks and shoulders as they got drunk, saying over and over how much they loved each other and how much fun they were having.

I saw my mother talking right in the middle of one of the groups. She was dressed in a flowing flower shirt and matching flower headband. My mom was beautiful, about 5'4" and thin with long sandy blond hair, ocean blue eyes, and a megawatt smile. She's always the life of the party and knows it, soaking in all the attention from everyone. A flower child and product of the peace, love, and drugs era, she seemed happy today. Her laugh cascaded through the crowd and fell on my ears. She turned to me. We locked eyes for just a moment. She smiled. I caught it with my heart and ran back to play as I heard my name being called by one of the other kids.

It was good to see her happy. She'd had a rough life and there were usually more tears than smiles. That is except for the weekends when Mom and Bruce would cut loose and let the euphoria of alcohol and drugs guide moods that kept them happy as long as there were people around.

Mom was abused as a child, too, and ran away at 15 years old. She moved to California to get away from the pain she was feeling. The pain kept her on a rollercoaster of emotions, ranging from sad to how I saw her now, being the life of the party.

She met Bruce after my father. He's been in my life since I was one. He stood about 6'2" tall, had long dark hair he kept in a ponytail, and a long beard that he would sometimes braid. He had huge, weathered hands and was in great physical shape due to working in construction. To me, Bruce was a true giant of a man. He was usually a brooding figure, quick to anger, and struck us at every opportunity. But at parties he seemed to settle in as the high of the drugs took away the pain he couldn't control.

I stood in the middle of the yard, taking it all in and looking around the smoky haze as the scenario played out in front of me. *Why can't life be more like this? Why can't we just be a happy family?*

I was shaken out of my trance just in time to see one of the older kids riding towards me on an ATV, yelling as he got close. I turned just in time to see the single headlight and red paint inches away from my face as I jumped out of the way, trying not to get run over. I felt the exhaust hit my leg when he passed by. The adults were high as a kite and laughed hysterically, watching the teenager chase all of us smaller kids through the yard, coming closer with every pass but turning just before we leapt to safety.

We hid behind trees and animal cages before sprinting across the yard and the patio where home base was, attempting to dodge the oncoming vehicle. The all-terrain tires were quickly deflating and half full, which caused the ATV to bounce like a balloon. The teen drove faster and finally crashed. The adults didn't seem to really care. Once his dad realized he wasn't hurt, he called the kid a dumbass and told him to go find something else to do.

The adults sat around the bonfire and in lawn chairs in the middle of the yard as it got dark. They reminisced about life, talking about their younger years, lost loves, and what could have been. The fire crackled loudly as each log of dry wood was added. Embers flew into the sky like twinkling lights and the nighttime summer breeze finally lifted the stifling heat of the day. All of us kids cooked our hotdogs over the open flame and drank straight from the hose when we were thirsty.

After dinner, I wanted to play *Star Wars* and yelled out to the other kids that we needed to split into teams for a battle. I grabbed the Millennium Falcon I'd made out of a cardboard box the week before. I stood in the middle of the box and grabbed the makeshift handles I'd cut into the sides, making sure to point the lights drawn with markers to the front. I pretended my spaceship was taking off after being docked and was ready to defend the galaxy. I ran towards the other kids who took the place of every character in the movie. We all became Han Solo, Luke Skywalker, Darth Vader, Princess Leia, and Chewbacca—all of us trying to lift our empire to power.

Making use of the entire yard, we ran around every inch of the entire half acre, making lightsaber and blaster sounds with our sticks. You could hear *hmmm*, *whoosh*, *pew pew*, and see each kid running full speed as we transported ourselves into the life of the movie. Lightsabers were especially brutal. The boys slapped the sticks together loud enough to hear them cracking against each other as they dueled. Tommy and I hit our sticks together and a shard hit him in the face when it broke. He ran crying to his mom, who told us all it was time to find another game to play.

We all groaned when she made us throw our lightsabers into the fire. I watched as the flames leapt from the fire, growing immediately bigger and bursting with embers as we threw our sticks into the flames.

One of the adults yelled out in a slurred voice, "You want to see a real fire kids?" He stumbled over to the grill, found a bottle of lighter fluid, and sprayed it into the fire.

A loud audible *whoosh* and fireball rose from the fire. I turned my head from the intense heat. All of the kids were mesmerized and watched the flicker of the light dancing off the reflection of our eyes.

One of the adults yelled, "Go back and play, but go get us all some fresh beers first." He continued, "Whoever gets back first gets a quarter."

Each of us raced to the cooler, pushing and jockeying for position to grab a beer from the frigid water. We reached into the bottom, knocking the cans out of each other's hands to ensure we had a chance of winning and getting the money. The rest of the night, I and the other kids played until we fell asleep on couches, floors or anywhere else we could find to rest our weary heads.

———

The next day, Bruce woke up and told Faith and I to go pick up the beer cans lying outside. We stepped out the door to see the aftermath two days of partying left behind. Hundreds of empty beer cans were all over the place. It was an absolute mess. There were cans on the tables, near the shed, on top of the animal cages, and all over the ground. It was obvious that, as the adults got more drunk, their aim was about as good as a blind man shooting a squirrel. It seemed like nobody even tried to get one in the trashcan.

Our backyard was huge, at least half of an acre that we'd turned into a mini farm. We had a few animals and grew vegetables in a garden. We surrounded the vegetables with a fence in the back corner so the animals wouldn't eat the food. Our brown and white goat, Billy, was my favorite animal. He had two small horns and a beard hanging from his chin that rivaled ZZ Top. He'd chase us, and we'd run from him, laughing while we sprinted away. He would let us pet him if we had food.

We also had two rabbits: one of them white with red eyes and the other black. They were used to us holding them and loved when we'd bring lettuce from the garden to eat, letting us pet them while they sat in our lap. They had the biggest front buckteeth and short fluffy tails. Their fur was soft like a fluffy cozy blanket and their huge feet propelled them across the yard with lightning speed.

In the very back of the yard, next to a tall cinder block wall, my mom and Bruce overgrew a giant swatch of weeds. The weeds were at least six feet tall with a clearing in the middle full of marijuana plants, leaving only the outside perimeter to hide its contents.

Faith and I were told to stay away from the path. The plants had the brightest green leaves and my mom had individual names for them. She'd tell us she was going to check on tooty fruity, juicy fruit, and blueberry crumble before disappearing behind the weeds. She'd return with bags of cut marijuana branches and place them upside down in the shed to dry.

I walked in the middle of the weeds to grab some of the trash and Faith yelled out to me, "Get out of there! You know we're not supposed to go anywhere near that. You want to get beat by Bruce?"

It was a stark reminder that I was in an off-limits area and better move quickly. I grabbed the remaining beer cans and we both ran back to the trash to throw the rest of the cans in. I wiped my hands on my shirt. The stale smell of warm beer wafted through my nose, almost making me sick. Faith and I looked up as we heard the screen door creek open, slamming shut with a loud bang as the wooden frame hit the door jam.

Bruce stepped out and surveyed the backyard. He wiped the sleep out of his eyes and stretched his arms up above his head, seemingly still in a daze from the night before. He wore his cut off denim shorts, no shirt, and pulled his long brown hair into a ponytail.

He stood there, looking into the backyard for what seemed like an eternity. We waited to see if we did a good enough job to be allowed to play. Then I saw the physical change in him as he suddenly became visibly agitated. Bruce shook his head back and forth in frustration and looked right at me.

"I thought I told you to pick up the beer cans from last night!"

I looked into the yard before speaking. I didn't see any cans, so I mumbled back in a light sheepish voice, "I did pick up the beer cans from last night."

He looked at me like a deranged lunatic and raised his voice, "I can't believe how stupid you are! Get over here, you fucking blind idiot."

He grabbed me by the arm and pushed my face down into a can I had accidentally left on the ground by the door. "Does this look clean to you? Huh? Does it?" He jerked me back on my feet and tightened his grip on my arm.

I felt a sense of dread. My heart leapt out of my chest, and I felt panic set in from knowing he was angry again. He opened the door to the house and pushed me inside, telling Faith to come in, too. He slapped the back of her head as she maneuvered past him.

He pushed us into the kitchen and yelled, "Look at all of the cans in here! Why didn't you pick these up? I said to pick up all of them."

My feet froze to the sticky beer dried on the floor, but I followed Faith's lead and desperately scrambled to pick up any can within reach. Neither of us realized we needed to pick up the cans *inside* of the house, but we both knew it was too late to do anything more, and that a beating was surely coming.

Faith and I locked eyes. We always knew what the other was thinking. This time my mind internally screamed for help and tried to find a way to get out of trouble. We said we would pick the rest up, but he told us it was too late. He ordered us to get a stick from the yard to get beat with.

We walked slowly to a tree, looking at the branches in the yard and trying to figure out which one would hurt least. I kept my head down and pretended that I was looking towards the ground. I studied each and every root, branch, and divot hoping he would go back inside or feel too hungover to beat us.

"Hurry up and find one before I do," Bruce snapped.

I picked up the skinniest branch I could find because I thought it would hurt less or maybe even break.

We gave him the stick and he pointed to the ping-pong table, telling us to assume the position. We'd had this happen before and knew it meant to lean against the table. The table was scraggly and its old, cracked top felt rough on my hands. I mentally prepared the best I could, trying to transport myself to another place, a place pain free and away from here.

"Put your hands on the edge," Bruce ordered. "And stick your ass out or I'll hit you in the back with it."

My eyes were level with the top of the table. I pushed my palms into the edge to brace myself and so my mouth didn't hit the side from the jolting smacks I knew were coming. I tried to be still on the first hit, hoping it would be the last one and maybe he'd stop. I definitely knew that, if I moved, I would feel the sting of the branch on any part of my body he could make contact with.

The whipping sound of the branch through the air gave me a millisecond of notice before the sting of the skinny branch hit me like the tip of a bullwhip. I gritted my teeth, squinted my eyes, and furrowed my face in preparation of the full impact. The branch whooshed through the air, snapping loudly as it hit my thin 1980s nylon shorts. The pain penetrated through the shorts and on my underwear like a hot iron. I felt my skin split open, causing a burning pain to take hold. My knees buckled immediately.

He struck me three times before switching to hit Faith. We looked at each other and tried to stay strong. He switched back to me and tried to hit me again, but this time I flinched and tried to block the stick with my hand, somehow thinking it would hurt less. I put my hand up towards the stick and covered my butt. The smack sounded even louder on my raw flesh and welted my skin immediately. The beating was unbearable. I started crying in pain, unable to take it any longer.

I prayed he would stop hitting me, but he continued the assault on my hands, butt, legs, and back until I collapsed in a ball on the patio, unable to stand any longer. This type of punishment, and beatings for anything Bruce felt like, were the norm in our house. There was nobody around to stop him when he decided to inflict pain on us.

Not too long after this incident, we ended up moving again.

"OK, kids, pack your shit up." Bruce yelled out to us one day when he came home from work.

He'd lost his job again and we couldn't afford our house anymore. We were moving to a much smaller place and told to only bring our inside toys and a few smaller ones from the outside because space was limited.

I felt sad because we were also told the animals I loved were going to be sold or given away. The animals provided a haven for me, a place I could use for escape and to find peace. I felt terrible when they were taken away and stared out the window of the living room while they were loaded up one by one.

Bruce and Mom shifted their focus to chopping down the marijuana plants they'd grown in the backyard, cleaning out the shed, and putting all of the cut up weed in large ziplock bags. They moved quickly, removing any evidence of drugs before we left, and burning anything they couldn't take with us. Even though I was only five, I knew what to do since we'd moved so much.

The turmoil was normal, and I got excited from "trying" a new place out and making more friends. I grabbed a heavy-duty black garbage bag and put my toys inside, making sure to grab every *GI Joe*, *Star Wars*, and *He-Man* toy I owned. They were precious to me, so I crawled under my bed and looked behind each piece of furniture until I was positive that I didn't leave any behind.

Mom set a box in the room, and I transferred my clothes from the small dresser, doing my best to hurry so I wouldn't get in trouble.

I asked Mom, "Are we going to have to move with the bad lady again?" Tears welled up in my eyes as bad memories flooded my brain.

Mom assured Faith and me that we were going with her. "We need to move into a smaller place because we don't have a lot of money, but we'll make it a great adventure full of fun and excitement."

We stayed in the same town but about 15 minutes from our previous house. This house was half the size with a much smaller backyard. Our new house wasn't on a main street in town like the other one, but instead in a neighborhood, which gave us a lot more freedom to roam around. I felt sad that the size of our backyard wouldn't allow us to have big parties anymore. It also meant we wouldn't get to see our friends again. I knew I'd just have to make the best of it.

———

Faith and I would wake up in the morning and ride our bikes through our entire side of town, coming back once it was dark to grab oranges from the orange tree in the backyard and lemon grass from our neighbor's yard because we were so hungry.

Even though my BMX bike was used, it was my ticket to freedom, so I took great care of it. I loved to pedal as fast as I could through the dirt driveway and slide the back tire through the dirt, trying to copy "The Dukes of Hazzard." I'd even sing the theme song, "Just Some Good Ol' Boys" out loud, doing my best to emulate Bo and Luke. The ability to ride wherever I wanted made the transition to another place much easier.

Mom was the most excited about the move because we were only one block away from her best friend, who was also our babysitter. The family had a son, Donny. He was a little older than me, but I got along with him really well and was thankful to have at least one friend in the new neighborhood. The mood in our new house felt somber. Mom and Bruce were easily agitated, especially on the weekends where we spent more time on our own instead of the large parties they were used to.

Mom and Bruce started hanging out with Donny's parents, Don and Cheryl, every weekend because they also liked to party. All of their marijuana and alcohol use increased significantly, and they also started to heavily use meth. We'd watch them snort it through a straw or smoke it through a pipe. They were fun when high, but they'd become extremely paranoid and skittish when coming down from their high. Bruce was especially quick to lash and strike us when detoxing.

Don and Cheryl's house had fluorescent yellow lighting and a sunk-in living room where everyone usually gathered. It was the only room with a TV. The rabbit ears on top were taped with tin foil for better reception, and each channel changed with a heavy clunking sound when we turned the knob. Inside of the house was dark brown wood paneling and orange shag carpeting straight out of the '70s.

I'd normally watch TV as the adults gathered around the coffee table. Don would reach under the couch and bring out a box that became a familiar site when we went to visit. It was a box made from wood and corners that dovetailed to create strong joints. It was about as big as a piece of paper and about as deep as a big book. It had a glass top emblazoned with a skull that had a straw sticking out of its nose. The top ran through grooves and slid out easily, uncovering the contents inside.

Don would set the top down next to the box on the coffee table. All of their eyebrows would lift, their eyes got bigger, and they became happier as they looked at the drugs inside. There were plastic bags of marijuana, rolling papers, methamphetamines, and pills all neatly placed in specific areas. I'd watch them, mesmerized by how joyful they seemed. They'd pull out the weed and put it into a silver machine, turning the handle and grinding it up into smaller chunks before putting it on the zig-zag paper. Bruce could roll a joint really fast and he'd always start by sprinkling the weed in the middle of the papers.

Cheryl reached over and turned up the music, blaring Lynyrd Skynyrd from the radio.

"Sweet Home Alabama," Mom and Cheryl sang out loud.

Mom and Cheryl sat on the couch and leaned in as they sang. Each one smiled from ear to ear and giggled in preparation for their first hit. They looked so happy. Their faces grew more excited as Bruce finished putting the weed on the rolling paper and licked the top to help it stick together. He grabbed a lighter and lit the joint. They all closed their eyes while taking a long drag. Puffy clouds of smoke filled the room. I studied each of their faces. It seemed like they held their breath for minutes before laughing or coughing and blowing the smoke in the direction of us kids on the floor.

The night carried on and, after knocking back a few beers and joints, I saw Cheryl take a small baggy, full of pure white powder, out of the box. They poured the powder onto a mirror with a skull on it. I couldn't help but think the powder reminded me of our white rabbits' fur as I stared at it. She took the queen of hearts from the card deck and tapped it on the glass. I heard Bruce say that it was time to really get this party started. I cocked my head to the side and watched in amazement as she broke the meth up into four distinct lines, smoothing and stretching each out.

Don grabbed a straw, cut it into three pieces with a pair of scissors, and put one in his nose. He pulled the mirror up to his face and buried the other end of the straw into the white powder. I watched as he inhaled deeply, making the powder disappear in one motion. He crunched up his nose and used his hand to move it from side to side because mucus was running down his nostrils. His eyes looked watery for a second, then he jumped up from the couch yelling, "Fuck yes!" while repeating how good the meth hit.

Cheryl, Mom, and Bruce all took turns snorting. I watched them fill with energy and get really hyper within seconds of taking it. Mom ran to the radio and bent over to turn it up louder. She turned her head back towards the group and began to almost scream the song out loud. Her blue eyes were as big as saucers and energy burst through her like a powerful and uncontrollable light.

Mom grabbed my hand, lifted me up off the floor, and told me to dance with her. We held hands and danced in circles, laughing the whole time. I felt great and jumped around until I got dizzy and fell down. It was a joyous moment. The adults had wild looks in their eyes and were grinding their teeth together. Donny, Faith, and I talked about how much fun it was when they snorted the white powder.

Myself and the other kids talked about trying it so we could be full of energy and excited like our parents.

CHAPTER 3
FIRST DAY OF SCHOOL

I started kindergarten a few months later. I was so excited to start school. It became my refuge; a place where Bruce couldn't hit me or call me names; a place where the teachers were nice to me; and the first place where I finally saw what normal looked like. Mom dropped us off at Cheryl's in the morning before she went to work to get ready for school. I liked going there in the morning because Cheryl was nice to us. She didn't work so she didn't mind helping Mom. They always had cocoa pebbles cereal, so I enjoyed starting my day out there.

I burst out of the front door when it was time to leave for school.

"Let's go!" I shouted, ready to start the day.

Donny, Faith, and I walked the six blocks to school together every day. I loved every minute of it. I felt grown up when we walked by ourselves, feeling in charge because I wasn't in the house being told what to do. I thought I was a big kid now doing big kid things.

I jumped off the steps and onto the concrete in my blue pro-wings shoes and favorite BMX shirt, ready to conquer the day. It was autumn, and the trees looked full, but were becoming multi-colored. The leaves changed from dark green, light yellow, and orange as fall adjusted the summer landscape, leaving us with chilly mornings and warm afternoons. I skipped and spun around on the sidewalk, full of energy and ready to go see my friends.

Just before the school, we passed a church, its giant cross dominating my view. I stared at the cross for a few minutes and, even though I'd never been in a church, the spirit felt familiar for some reason. In big block letters across the middle of the church it read "First Presbyterian Church." The church was freshly painted white, with multiple buildings attached to the chapel and grounds. The building walkways were concrete paths bordered by the greenest fescue grass. Beautiful lilies, daisies, and other multi-colored flowers were strewn across the front, neatly placed near the building and in pots throughout the courtyard.

In the courtyard was a giant cast iron, extremely heavy bell. It had a small loop welded into the bottom so the clergy could ring it on Sunday. The bell captured our attention as we walked by. I felt like it was sitting there by itself, calling our names, and begging to be rung. Faith even dared me to ring it!

Donny egged me on, too. "Come on! Don't be a Wilma. Just do it."

Man, I hated when people called me Wilma. It was the pet name from Bruce and Mom because I was scared a lot of the time.

They'd say, "You're so scared all the time, just like a girl. We're going to keep calling you Wilma from now on until you figure out how to get tougher and stop crying."

Bruce especially liked to use it after he hit me and I was crying in pain, telling me to "Keep crying, Wilma. You piece of shit."

I was pissed that Donny and Faith called me Wilma. I didn't want to let fear stop me from doing something anymore. I didn't want them to keep making fun of me, either, especially for something as easy as ringing a bell.

I was scared, but I wanted to hear how loud the bell would be, so I decided to ring it. My heart raced and I walked back and forth on the sidewalk, attempting to muster up the courage to go for it. My mind contemplated all the reasons why I could do it: I could run fast enough to not get caught; There was enough concrete that I wouldn't slip running away; Our school was right next door so all I had to do was run inside the doors of the school after I rang it to get away.

Every possible action plan ran through my head as I psyched myself up. I made the decision, and moved from fear to action, sprinting to the bell as fast as my legs could carry me, looking around frantically and hoping nobody was watching.

I pushed the outside of the bell with all my might, but it didn't move an inch. It was so heavy and felt like pushing against a brick wall. I looked back to see Faith and Donny watching, laughing and pointing towards me, slapping their knees at the hilarity in front of them. My face turned red with embarrassment. I felt weak and my brain screamed out in frustration.

"C'mon, dang it!" I yelled out, knowing I had to find a way to ring the bell or else be ridiculed for weeks by both of them.

As a last resort, I stuck my finger in the loop at the bottom and pulled with every ounce of strength I had, rocking myself back off the concrete bench I was standing on. The bell started to move towards me, so I yanked on it with one last desperate effort. The cast iron felt like 200 pounds and I felt like I needed the strength of ten men to keep it going. The bell reached its peak and I tried to let go, but the momentum pulled me downward. I tried pulling my finger from the loop again and it wouldn't budge. *Oh crap*, I thought to myself, *How am I going to get out of this?!*

The bell's momentum was unstoppable due to the weight. It yanked my arm down and almost pulled me onto the platform as it swung away from me. There was nothing I could do to stop it. My eyes widened as I desperately pulled and pulled on my finger until it finally became unstuck. The bell banged into the clapper and kept swinging, returning its momentum back down towards the clapper a second time and ringing so loudly it made me a bit dizzy.

The sound was deafening. I ran as fast as the Roadrunner being chased by Wile E. Coyote through the church grounds and towards Faith and Donny who were already running in front of me. I didn't turn around to even look, because I felt it might slow me down and I didn't want someone from the church to see my face. Faith, Donny, and I laughed hysterically as we busted through the doors of the school, finally out of eyesight and potential trouble. All of us smiled from ear to ear and breathed heavily; the adrenaline, fear, and now joy took hold of us all at one time.

I yelled out, "That was awesome! Holy mackerel, it was loud!" Faith gave me a high five before we all went to class.

———

From that day on, we'd stop at the church and ring the bell on our way to school, looking to replicate the excitement just one more time.

Halfway through kindergarten, and after many times running through the church grounds, Donny pointed to the roof and said we should see what was on top. We didn't ever go on the roof, but it was easily accessible. There was a staircase leading to the second floor offices that gave us access to the adjacent first floor office roof.

We'd realized that nobody was ever at the church by 7:30 in the morning, so we started to explore and made the building our own jungle gym. We'd all run up the stairs and jump onto the roof. It was a large area and had plenty of places to hide due to the air conditioner units on top. The early morning sunrise glimmered off the large silver air conditioning condensers. Once on the roof, nobody could see us behind the AC units. It became like our own personal fort.

After a few months, Faith brought Marlboro Red cigarettes and a lighter from Mom's purse with her to the church. She said we should see what it was like to smoke since our parents smoked every day and they seemed to enjoy it.

We did like it and started to smoke on the rooftop every day before school. We knew we couldn't keep taking Mom's packs because she'd find out we were stealing them. We also knew she'd tell Bruce and we'd get beat for stealing, so we started picking cigarette butts off the ground and smoking them. I felt like smoking was gross and made me stink, but I wanted to be cool, so I kept doing it.

Faith, Donny, and I started to get bored with smoking, so we talked about trying the white powder. We reminisced about the euphoria and outburst of energy we'd seen from our parents and how they were so much fun when they used meth. Our parents snorted meth every weekend, even sometimes during the week. Their energy after doing it was something we all wanted to feel. So, we made a plan to take some. Donny said he thought he could take the meth without getting caught.

The final month of school arrived and Cheryl reminded us that we only had four weeks left of our morning ritual. I couldn't wait to finish the year. Faith, Donny, and I all talked about summertime over breakfast. Donny excused himself while we were eating cereal and came back into the kitchen telling us that we needed to go now. I didn't know why he was so rushed all of a sudden but followed along.

Donny seemed anxious while we played our daily game of trying to avoid all the cracks on the sidewalk. We jumped from slab to slab and leapt over cracked tree roots.

Faith sang out, "Step on a crack, break your momma's back."

Faith and I were really competitive, so we continued the game, playing the entire way until we made it to the church.

Donny took a full scan of the church grounds when we walked up, looking side to side to make sure nobody was around. He quietly whispered that we weren't going to ring the bell today because he had something better. We scurried up the stairs and made our way behind one of the giant silver condenser units.

Donny's voice cracked with excitement when he told us that he took one of the bags of white powder. He told us that Mom almost caught him as he slid the skull box back under the couch and he had to fake that he was looking for a lost shoe.

He pulled the meth out of his coat pockets and showed us the small ziplock baggie. We were all pumped to finally try it. It looked just like the same stuff our parents inhaled in their nose that made them jump around and gave them energy to do anything they wanted. Donny told me to set my He-Man Castle of Greyskull lunchbox on the ground. I complained because I didn't want to get it dirty. The lunchbox was metal with bright pictures on each side. It was my favorite lunchbox and I kept it in pristine condition. He-Man was my hero, and I knew he wouldn't want drugs on the lunchbox.

"I don't want to use my lunchbox," I said.

"We need something flat and out of the wind. If we put it on the air conditioners people can see us."

I reluctantly placed it on the ground. He took a piece of paper from his three-ring Trapper Keeper notebook, set it on top of my lunchbox, and carefully placed the powder on top of it. The powder was white and fluffy like a newly fallen snow. It was heavy enough to not fly away in the slight breeze, but still easy to make into lines.

He took out a playing card, just like we saw our parents do, and began to tap it on the paper, using long strokes to spread the meth out into three distinct long lines. The chemical smell hit my nose immediately. I turned my head away from it and ripped a piece of paper out of my notebook. I rolled up the paper into a straw, just like we saw our parents do many times before.

We all stopped for a moment and confirmed we were really going to snort it. Donny, Faith, and I looked at each other with wild eyes and a sense of eagerness that only comes from doing something you're not supposed to.

I stuck the paper in my nose. It tickled at first. My knees were getting uncomfortable because of the tiny pebbles pushing into them from the roof so I quickly bent down. I exhaled a deep breath, and then quickly inhaled while snorting the line of white powdered meth until it disappeared.

My nose felt like it was on fire, a chemical taste dripped into my throat as I grabbed my nose and closed my eyes in pain. I tried to wiggle my nose with my hand back and forth like I'd seen my mom and Bruce do, but it didn't help.

It hit me like a ton of bricks, working into my bloodstream fast and furiously, surging adrenaline through my body and making me feel like I was on a rocket ship headed for the moon. The nerves in my body shot through me like million strikes of lightning, my heartbeat so fast I felt it pulsating in my neck. My jaw clenched together uncontrollably.

I leapt up. My eyes struggled to see. I squinted at the sun. The school bell rang, and the rush of energy was so insurmountable that I jumped down multiple steps at a time from the church roof. I stopped at the edge of the church grounds, feeling instantly ravished and ready to eat. I unclipped the front of my lunch box, finding a peanut butter and jelly sandwich with a small bag of Lays potato chips inside, and devoured all of it immediately while my body continued to operate in overdrive.

I couldn't control what I was feeling or any of this energy seemingly pushing out of my chest like a giant ray of light. I felt like ripping off my clothes, jumping to the roof of the school, flying past my classmates, and running in circles. I couldn't stop it!

I sat in class. My feet rapidly tapped on the floor. I felt Ms. Grey look my way until she finally asked me to sit quietly. I sat there watching the clock and tried to stay out of trouble. My eyes darted around the room and my mind spun out of control until the last recess bell rang. The incredible energy I'd felt at the beginning of the day seemed to instantly drain from my body and I was exhausted from trying to keep my composure all day.

I put my head on my school desk and tried to close my eyes. Ms. Grey asked me what was wrong, and I told her I wasn't feeling well. She told me to go to the nurse's office. The nurse took my temperature, which came back normal. She told me to rest in the nurse's bed until the school day was over. I was happy because I felt like I couldn't move my body anymore anyway. My mind continued to race as I laid there, and the rest of the day felt like a blur as I came crashing down from my high.

I knew I would never try and take another line of meth again because I felt so terrible. Faith and Donny said the same. We were tired, weak, aggravated, and hated how we felt. We made a commitment to each other to stay away from the drugs in the skull box from that day forward.

CHAPTER 4
KIDNAPPED

The school receptionist called me to the office one day and told me that my parents were in the building and picking me up for the day. I was confused because my mom didn't say anything about getting us early from school. Faith walked across the tree-lined courtyard towards me. She said she didn't know anything about getting picked up today and we started wondering if something bad happened. We walked down the main sidewalk together and towards the office. We were perplexed and thinking about what could have happened to make Mom come get us.

A man all dressed in black leaned against a tree and said, "Hey, Faith and Walt, Jr." He waved at us when we walked past.

I was only six years old at this time. Mom told us constantly not to go with strangers, so I didn't say anything. I just stared at him for a minute before running into the office with Faith. I thought I heard him say he was my uncle, but we pushed through the double doors and didn't turn around to make sure.

The principal met us just inside and asked us to follow him to a conference room. In the conference room was my dad and a lady I'd never met. I had a confused look on my face because I didn't recognize my dad after not seeing him in years.

My dad looked at us, smiled, and said, "Hey, Walt and Faith, I'm your dad."

I was shocked and stood there in disbelief because I didn't know him. The last time I saw him I was two years old and we had only lived together for a little bit. Faith seemed to remember him, but I was bewildered. The principal assured us that he was our father and we were OK leaving with him today. I felt uneasy and wondered where Mom was and if she knew Dad was here.

They planned to take us back to San Diego with them and, since there was no custody arrangement between my parents, each one could get us anytime they pleased. My dad's girlfriend, Gail, walked up and introduced herself to us. I looked at her belly. She told me she was pregnant with my little brother and that we would get to meet him in a few months.

Dad said, " I know you're scared, but everything is going to be OK. We're going to be a happy family now."

Faith asked if we were going to be able to get our clothes and toys and he said we would buy new ones when we got back to San Diego.

He led us out of the office, and we started to make our way down the sidewalk and to the parking lot. None of this made sense to me. My mind screamed out in confusion. I felt like he was kidnapping us and taking us from the only parent we knew. I kept looking up at my dad as we walked across the parking lot. I felt a sense of familiarity, which was slightly calming, but most of my being was swarming with chaos. I wondered what was going to happen to us and was scared about what was next.

I looked back down towards the ground, my mind in a fog, confused and still not understanding what was happening. I then looked back towards the office and saw my mom running between two trees and straight towards us. She was yelling and wildly waving her arms in the air. She'd found out that Dad was there to get us and was trying to stop it. The school police officer and my uncle stepped in front of my mother as she got closer and blocked her from getting to us.

My dad squeezed our hands tighter and walked faster towards the car. I kept looking at my dad, then my mom. The emotion of the moment was stifling, and I was confused with who we were supposed to go with.

I yelled out for her. "Mom!! Mom, please help us." I was terrified we were being taken away and felt paralyzed with fear.

I saw the sun hit her face, clearly showing the look of helplessness. Tears flowed from her blue eyes as her kids were taken away. There was nothing she could do about it. The officer restrained her as she stretched her arms in our direction, reaching for Faith and me in a thwarted attempt to get to us.

My dad opened the door and lifted the front seat so Faith and I could get in the back. I cried and yelled out the back window as Mom ran towards the car. I tried to reach for her and placed my hand on the back window. I watched her sprint through the parking lot as we sped away. Hands on her knees, she panted in desperation and looked towards our direction until we disappeared. Dad and Gail kept telling us that it was going to be OK and we'll be happier with them in San Diego.

———

The ride back to San Diego was quiet and long. Faith and I just looked at each other, unsure of what was coming or where San Diego even was. It might as well have been a world away in my mind. Dad tried to break the silence by telling us about the apartment they lived in. He said it was only ten miles from the beach and we would go whenever we wanted. He told us how much fun living in a bigger city like San Diego was. He told us there was so much to do and did his best to alleviate our fear.

Dad seemed like a really nice guy so far. Part of me was relieved we wouldn't have to live with Bruce anymore. Dad really got into his storytelling and narrated tales about the beaches, the San Diego Zoo, Balboa Park, and watching planes at the airport. He was a great storyteller and made each place seem enthralling and enticingly vibrant. I still couldn't really make sense of the tornado of emotions inside of me, but part of me felt like San Diego could be fun.

———

We stopped at a McDonald's on the way and went inside to eat. Dad told us how much of a treat it was to have us back and how he looked forward to this day for a long time. He asked me if I wanted a happy meal since they had toys in them. Of course, I said yes. I ate the chicken nuggets and small fry as he told us more stories about his time in the Army and how he met Gail. Dad and Gail talked about how exciting it was to add another boy to the family and, with everyone together, life would be complete. He carried on and said how great of a big brother and sister he thought Faith and I would be.

We walked into the apartment; it was small with only two bedrooms. Faith and I followed him into the bedroom. The room had bunk beds right next to the door on the other side of the room from the window. There were passenger model airplanes hanging from fishing lines on the ceiling. I thought it looked really cool because it seemed like they were flying through the air.

He asked me, "Jr., do you know any of the planes?"

He took down a 747 jumbo jet, his favorite, and handed it to me so I could get a closer look. He said it was the first model he'd built, and we would build some together to fill the rest of our mini airport.

I tried to be happy as Faith and I talked in bed that night, both of us checking to make sure the other was OK. I told Faith I was scared, and she told me not to worry. She said she'd protect me and, as long as we were together, we'd be OK. I went through such a range of emotions over the next few weeks as I tried to acclimate to my new surroundings. I felt like I was floating through the air and everything was cloudy. It would take time to get to know this stranger, my father.

The first couple of months of living with Dad were amazing. He didn't yell or hit us like Bruce did. Instead, he'd have fun with us by taking Faith and I to experience San Diego. He told us he loved us, which took some getting used to. I started to feel better about moving in with him.

Our favorite thing to do at the house was play catch. He bought two paddle catch games for us to "practice" baseball in the house. For hours, I would stand in the kitchen and throw the fuzzy tennis ball back and forth with Dad, the flat Velcro gloves sticking to the ball making it easy for me to catch. He told me I was getting great quickly and that soon I'd be able to play T-ball in the city league. Baseball was my dad's favorite sport and, if I was good enough, I knew he would love me even more.

———

Summer finally came, and I couldn't wait to go to the pool. I desperately wanted to learn how to swim, especially because we'd go to the beach so much, but was terrified to go into the deep end. Dad would sit under the umbrella in the shade smoking his Marlboro Red cigarettes or joint while drinking a beer. He rarely got in the water. I'd hold onto the sides of the pool when I couldn't reach the bottom. Dad tried to talk me into swimming from side to side, but the fear of drowning kept me tentative.

After a couple of weeks at the pool, he told me he was going to teach me the "old school" way to swim. I didn't know what that meant, but I was excited for him to teach me how to quit sinking.

I heard Gail tell him, "You better not do what I think you're about to do," as we entered the gate to the pool.

He told me to walk to the edge with him and asked if I was ready. *Ready for what?* He grabbed me by my arms and threw me into the middle of the deep end. My head immediately went under the water, and I wildly flapped my arms, terrified I was going to drown. Gail jumped in the pool to help, but Dad told her to leave me for a minute.

I gulped water, unable to breathe, just as Gail pulled me to the surface and into the shallow end. I gasped for air, trying to catch my breath. Dad knelt down by the edge. "Son, you can reach now so calm down. The other edge isn't very far, right? I know you're strong enough to swim over there, but you won't be able to do it if you are scared in your head. Give it another try and if you get tired, stand up."

I was initially pissed off, but I wanted to try again. I was ready this time! I tucked my knees and used my feet to propel myself off the wall. I focused on the end point and kept kicking until my hand finally touched the other side.

Dad ran to the other side while I was swimming and gleefully said, "I told you that you could do it! Doesn't it feel great knowing you can? There was no way I was going to let you drown but I couldn't let fear stop you from pushing yourself and keeping you from enjoying the entire pool the rest of summer."

I was elated that I was able to get to the other side. I spent the rest of the summer enjoying the pool. It was a valuable lesson on pushing through fear and not letting your mind hold you back from obtaining your goals.

———

Dad loved to wake us up in the middle of the night to hang out with him. It didn't matter if it was a school night or the middle of summer, he figured kids could recover fast if we didn't get enough sleep.

Dad would sneak into my room and lightly tap my arm, excitedly saying, "Midnight snacky time," while rustling me out of bed to hang out.

I always woke up because it was time for just the two of us and he was at his happiest when we did this. We would have a different snack every time, but his favorites were Little Debbie Suzie-Q cakes, popcorn, candy, or corn-on-the-cob. I liked all of those things, too. We'd watch the latest episode of Fraggle Rock and cuddle on the couch while eating our snacks. Once the show was over, he'd tell me to head back to bed and give me a hug goodnight.

These moments were special to me, and I felt like the most important kid in the world when we did them. Those months were the best memories I have of my father. He taught me important life lessons and spent quality time with us. I felt loved, special, and important. Gail and Dad got along relatively well and, although they would argue and fight, we didn't see too much of it.

Gail and Dad seemed like they were in a good, mentally healthy space, but the stress of having a baby, increased drug use, and alcohol were going to change everything.

CHAPTER 5
A NEW ADDITION

A few months passed, and it got closer to my brother being born. Dad talked about how excited he was to have another little boy and how I'd need to be a responsible big brother. He brought home a crib for the baby, and we built it together, taking care to ensure we followed the directions and built it as sturdy as possible. Faith and I were told we'd share a room with our newborn brother, Patrick, since there wasn't any extra space in the apartment. Dad also told us they'd probably keep him in the bassinet in their room at first. We were prepped and ready for the new addition to the family, and only waiting for the delivery.

———

Not too long after, one early afternoon, Gail told Dad that she was having contractions. We all jumped for joy. The delivery day finally arrived. Patrick was coming! Dad called my uncle to come watch us and headed to the hospital with Gail.

It seemed like forever before they came home. The next day, Gail and Dad walked through the door. My dad was in a great mood and sang a silly song about bringing a baby home. Both Gail and Dad beamed with pride and were really happy.

Dad showed me the San Diego Padres onesie Patrick was wearing and said that we had to start him off right by making him a fan of the best baseball team in Major League Baseball.

Faith and I were pumped to meet Patrick. I wanted to hold my little brother for the first time. Gail bent down and placed him in the cradle of my arms. I stared at him in awe. I'd never held a baby before but I knew I would be his protector and help keep him safe.

———

I loved to play with Patrick. I played peek-a-boo with him every day until he'd give me his huge baby smile, which was my favorite.

Sports were always on the TV in our house. If Dad wasn't watching the San Diego Padres baseball team, we'd watch the San Diego Chargers football team. Dad would get so into the games sometimes that he'd yell at the TV in elation or disappointment, sometimes even waking Patrick up. His passion for sports spilled over to us kids because we knew it made him happy.

Dad loved sports memorabilia and told me we were going to start collecting baseball cards, saying they'd be worth a lot of money someday. He'd take Faith and I to the corner store to buy beer every day and we'd get to buy a pack of Topps baseball cards when we went with him. He taught me to open each package with care to ensure I didn't bend the edges or they'd lose their value. I didn't really care about the value, but I loved to eat the rock-hard gum that was inside the package.

Dad and I would sit on the floor and separate each card by team, putting each player in alphabetical order. Dad bought a special case that held hundreds of cards. We'd meticulously place each of them in the case in the same order we had them on the floor, putting them away for the day we could make a lot of money selling them. Dad told me to make sure I gave them to my kids one day and, if they were ever worth as much as a Babe Ruth card, we'd be rich.

Dad and Gail's drug use seemed to massively increase from recreational to full-on addiction after Patrick was born. They moved from just marijuana and alcohol to prescription pills and meth, which escalated their volatility and fighting.

Patrick was an extremely cute, but fussy, baby and I noticed the mood in the house began to change. Dad and Gail fought in their bedroom more than usual. They would be so loud that Faith and I heard every word clearly. Over time, they began fighting in front of us because Dad would leave to go get drunk at the bar and they'd be yelling as he walked out of the apartment.

The drinking and drugs were out of control for both of them and the tension in the house became so thick you could cut it with a knife. One day, Dad ripped open the door of their bedroom. Gail was on his heels, screaming at the top of her lungs.

They were both exceptionally angry. I saw scratches on my dad's face and a hand mark on Gail's. I'd never seen them hit each other before that day, only heard it, but this time neither of them were holding back. Gail was a tall, athletically built woman with long brown hair and brown eyes. At 5'9", she was the same height as my dad and could hold her own against him, which escalated the level of violence immensely.

Gail yelled about my dad's drinking and marijuana use. Dad was pissed about finding meth in Gail's underwear drawer. Gail threw a cup at Dad and he kicked her in the stomach, knocking her to the ground. She ran into the room and grabbed a bat before running at my dad and hitting him in the side with it.

He punched her in the face, knocking her down to the ground again. Her eye almost immediately swelled shut. Faith and I stared wide-eyed and hid behind the couch.

Dad told her to get the fuck out and left the house, slamming the door behind him, and headed to the bar to get drunk. Gail yelled at Faith and I to go to our room and not come out again the rest of the night.

———

As the abuse between the two of them escalated, Gail's anger with my dad spilled over to Faith and I. She became more physically abusive, taking every opportunity to transfer the pain she felt to me because it would piss Dad off.

She became increasingly paranoid from the meth use and even accused me of working with the police and Dad to have her arrested. Dad started to lash out more at me, too, slapping me for things like not keeping my toys picked up. He became more abusive with each beer he drank. I hated alcohol for making him so angry. Faith and I tried to steer clear of both of them and played outside as much as possible, but the apartment quickly became my prison as the abuse from both of them became insufferable.

Gail called me in the kitchen first thing in the morning and started to yell at me. "How many times do I have to tell you to clean your dishes after you use them? Why is there milk still in your cereal bowl?!"

She grabbed my arm and yanked me to the front of the sink, hollering in my ear so loud that my ears started ringing. "You're just like your father! He can't pick up after himself, either!" She twisted my arm and hurt me. I pulled my arm away, which made her even madder.

"I'm sorry. I'll clean the bowl right now. You're hurting me."

Gail replied, "I'm not taking the disrespect from your dad any longer and I'm damn sure not taking it from you, either." She reached over and poured a scalding hot cup of water directly from the coffee pot.

I was scared. I didn't know what she would do next. I sensed her anger growing by the second. "What are you going to do with the boiling water?"

She put the cup into my hand. "Drink it, now." She stared at me with blank angry eyes.

I almost dropped the cup. The outside was scalding hot. "I can't hold it. It's too hot."

This enraged her. She reared her hand back and smacked me in the face. "When I'm done with you, you'll never talk back to me again!" She pushed the cup up to my face and grabbed a spatula off the counter. I started to say something and she popped me in the mouth with the spatula, causing me to reel back in pain and spill some of the hot water on the floor.

She grabbed my cheeks and squeezed them together, lowering her voice and saying to me, "Drink the water and, if you don't drink it, I'm going to hurt you."

I looked back at the cup. Steam rose off the water. I cried uncontrollably and tried to tell her it was going to burn me and really hurt. I contemplated running out the front door but knew it would be worse if she caught me.

Gail struck me with the spatula again and held it above her head to hit me again. "I'm not going to tell you again. You drink it or else."

It was like she wasn't even herself anymore. Like she was possessed. My dad and Faith had gone to the store. I knew that if I didn't drink it, she was going to beat me until I did. I grabbed the handle of the cup and felt the heat hit my face as I lifted it close to my mouth. Gail grabbed the bottom of the cup and tipped it the rest of the way up to my mouth.

The water poured out of the cup and onto my face, immediately causing burns and blisters on my lips. I dropped the cup and my body fell to the floor. The cup shattered as it hit the ground. My screams startled Patrick, who also started to scream. His screams seemed to knock Gail from her rage. She grabbed Patrick from his bassinet and stormed off to her room, leaving me writhing in pain on the ground until Dad got home.

When he walked in he asked why I was on the floor and what the hell happened. I told him that Gail made me drink boiling water.

Dad looked closely at my lips. "You'll be fine. Stop crying about it and toughen up. What did you do to deserve that, anyway?"

I didn't have anything to say and couldn't really talk because my lips were so swollen. Dad stood there for a minute then stormed off towards the bedroom. We heard Gail and him immediately start fighting.

Faith grabbed a popsicle from the freezer and told me to put it on my lips. She helped me clean up the broken mug and water on the floor.

I started crying and asked Faith, "Why does this keep happening?" I knew that neither of us had the answer.

We went and hid in our bedroom for the rest of the night. We didn't know how violent things between Dad and Gail were going to get, especially since we could hear them hitting each other in the next room.

My lips were blistered and more swollen the next day.

Gail looked at me for a minute. "You aren't allowed to go outside to play until your mouth heals."

Dad piped in, "We don't need someone calling Child Protective Services, so you better not go outside."

I knew they felt bad about what happened because I was allowed to eat all of the ice cream and popsicles I wanted until my mouth healed. They were also really nice to Faith and me over the next month. They told me we'd be back in foster homes if I said anything at school. They also said I would get something special for my birthday if I kept it secret.

I didn't want to end up in a foster home, so I never said anything.

———

A few weeks later, Dad announced that he was taking us to Disney on Ice for my seventh birthday. I was really excited to get out of the house and do something special, especially since I was cooped up while my lips healed.

We all loved Disney and my dad did a great job hyping up the show. He told us that we might even get to meet Mickey Mouse. I really liked when Dad was in a great mood. It instantly made me feel happy and loved. I knew that as long as he was happy, we weren't going to get beat, and he was a lot of fun when he joked around.

We parked and I looked around at all of the kids running towards the door. I awed at the way parents looked at their kids so lovingly and how excited their kids were for the show. The kids' excitement was contagious and filled me with so much joy.

The ice looked huge! The characters leapt, spun, crashed on purpose for a laugh, and waved at the crowd, creating an amazing show that transported me to another time and place for at least a couple of hours.

During the show, Dad seemed to be increasingly frustrated with Gail as she kept getting up from her seat to use the bathroom.

One of the times, he pushed his hand over her top lip and said, "You have white shit all over your face. I can't believe you're doing that here."

Gail smacked his hand away and told him to fuck off.

The ride home went from the euphoric intoxication to a tense argument between Dad and Gail that finally blew up as we passed over the mountains.

Gail was agitated from doing a line of meth and yelled at Dad. "You're worthless and ruining my high! I should have left you a long time ago. You're such a loser."

Dad yelled back. "Shut the fuck up or I'll leave you on this mountain!" His tone grew louder each time he said it.

Dad looked at Gail, which caused him to swerve into oncoming cars and almost caused a crash. Gail was in a rage and started to push Dad's whole body, forcing him to hit his head against the driver's side window. Dad slammed on the breaks. I wasn't ready for it to jerk me forward and my face hit the back of the passenger's seat. My eyes watered from the impact. I saw Dad grab Gail by the hair on the back of her head.

He pulled her head back then bounced her face off the dash, causing her nose to explode. I was terrified so I wedged myself behind the passenger seat on the floor and covered my face with my hands. She grabbed her face and let out a loud scream. Her hands filled up almost immediately with blood and got it all over the seat and dash.

"Get the fuck out of the car, bitch!" Dad yelled at her while he pushed her out the passenger door.

Gail jumped out of the car. "I'm going to call the police, you son of a bitch!"

Dad stomped on the gas. The tires squealed and her door slammed shut. He left her on top of the mountain pass in the dark. I heard the tires hit the rumble strips on the side of the road as Dad lost control of the vehicle while looking in the rear view mirror. He knew Gail would call the police and that he'd be arrested, so he decided we weren't going home.

He looked at Faith, Pat, and I in the back. "How about we go stay in a hotel tonight? We can buy some snacks and watch a movie. How does that sound, kids?"

We knew to nod our heads, but my mind just wanted to run as far away as possible. The violence between Dad and Gail was getting out of hand. It continued to spill over to us. I was afraid of how she'd take it out on me when given another opportunity.

Gail never called the police. The two of them tried to work it out, but ultimately split up a few months later. Gail brought her brother and his friends when she moved out. She didn't want to risk Dad hurting her while she got her stuff.

She cleaned out her personal belongings and most of the furniture from the apartment, which left it pretty empty. She told us to hug Patrick goodbye when she was done, and then they left.

It would be a few years before I saw Patrick again. Faith and I were about to be on the move, too. We just didn't know it yet.

CHAPTER 6
DUMPED ON THE SIDEWALK

Dad knew we couldn't afford to live in our apartment on his salary alone. We were on the brink of homelessness, so he decided a few months before my eighth birthday to take Faith and I back to Mom. He didn't tell us or anyone else about his plan. We left San Diego and headed North on I-15. Dad was silent. I could tell we were leaving the city limits, so I asked him where we were going. He didn't tell us, but instead tried to build excitement by saying it was a surprise. Almost two hours later, we arrived at a house in Hemet, California.

We pulled up to the front of the house and Dad stopped the car on the curb. He told Faith and I to get out of the car and go knock on the door. We were confused why he wasn't getting out and stared at him for a few seconds. We weren't even sure whose house this was.

He looked at both of us sternly and raised his hand up towards the back seat before yelling, "NOW! I said to get out! You're your mother's problem now. See if she wants you because I'm done with both of you."

Dad sat waiting in his car, with the engine still running, waiting for us to leave. We reluctantly exited the car and knocked on the door. Mom opened the door with a surprised look on her face. She stumbled over her words. "How did you two get here?"

"Dad brought us." I pointed back to the street towards his car.

Dad casually sat in the car. He kept his left hand on the wheel and leaned over to the passenger side, saying something incoherent out of the window to Mom. Mom couldn't hear him, so she stepped out of the tattered, ripped screen and started walking towards him. She interrupted him and asked what he was doing, dropping us off with nothing.

Dad yelled from the car, "They're your problem now! I can't take care of them anymore."

Faith and I stood there in total shock, never considering Dad was going to leave us somewhere. Mom stood there next to us, halfway between the front door and Dad's car. Dad stared at all of us for a couple of seconds but didn't say another word. He peeled out of the dirt in front of the house and took off down the street without as much as a goodbye.

Mom turned back to walk inside, leaving Faith and I standing in place, staring at each other and wondering what the heck just happened. We didn't have anything, not even the normal black heavy-duty garbage bags of clothes and the few toys we'd normally get to move with. I felt like a piece of garbage thrown away. My shoulders slumped over. I knew we were starting all over again. Faith grabbed my hand and we walked to the front door where Mom was standing.

Mom motioned for us to come inside and tried to cheer us up. "You guys are back just in time. We're moving to Indiana in a few weeks."

"We're moving again? Why Indiana?" The shock that we were living with her now, much less moving to an entirely different part of the country, shocked me.

"Bruce and I've been planning this for a long time now. I want to be closer to my family and all of them live there so they can help us out, too. Bruce already got a job and you kids will love living closer to your cousins."

I saw movement out of the corner of my eye. My little sister, Nicole, crawled over to me and my attention diverted to her. It was well over a year since we'd seen her, but I remember the day Mom brought Nicole home. Faith and I were so excited we had a little sister. I thought she looked so cute in her pink butterfly pajamas when she came home from the hospital. I remembered the first time Mom asked me if I wanted to hold her. Mom told me to sit on the couch as she carefully put her in my arms, her tiny hands and feet so precious and cute. She cooed and smiled as I played peek-a-boo and made funny faces at her. It was the cutest little grin and my heart smiled as big as my mouth did when I would get a reaction.

"Nicole is getting really big," I told Mom as she sat back down on the couch.

"She sure is, Walter, and she's also going to love having her big brother and sister home again."

Mom handed Nicole to me and walked into the kitchen with her hands in an attempt to gain her composure. After a few minutes, she came back out and asked if we were hungry or thirsty. I was hungry since we didn't get to eat on the drive. I was also really thirsty. The commotion and uncertainty gave me extreme cottonmouth.

Mom went into the kitchen to make us some peanut butter and jelly sandwiches and filled up some glasses of water while Faith and I took turns holding Nicole.

Mom told us over lunch that Faith and I were going to ride with Bruce in the U-Haul while Nicole and her flew to Indiana. I still had terrible memories of Bruce, so I was shocked and nervous. I didn't want to be on a cross-country drive with him knowing what he was capable of.

I asked Mom why she wasn't going to ride with us. She told me that there isn't room for all five of us in the U-Haul, plus Nicole was too little to make a drive from California to Indiana. Mom told us it would be a fun adventure and we'd get a chance to see America. She also talked to us about her family, telling us how much we'd love living close to our grandparents, uncles, aunts, and cousins.

———

We set off on an early summer morning. The sweltering heat and humidity of inland southern California beamed the sun through the blue bird sky and warmed the cab of the U-Haul. It was already warm, and the U-Haul's air conditioner barely kept the cab cool as we started our drive. The cab was cramped with all three of us sharing one bench seat. Bruce drove, I sat in the middle, and Faith sat in the passenger's seat. Bruce told us at the beginning of the trip that we would drive until he needed to rest, and the goal was to be in Indiana within three days. We also wouldn't stay at any hotels because we didn't have the money.

On the first night, we drove fourteen hours all the way to Albuquerque before pulling into a rest stop to sleep. Bruce told Faith and I that we were going to sleep on the hood of the truck while he slept in the cab since there wasn't room for all three of us inside.

We pulled into a parking spot and grabbed some sandwiches, chips, and water from the cooler. It was dark except for the yellow light emanating from the streetlights lining the rest stop. Huge bugs flew around the lights. I was glad it also lit up the concrete path to the bathrooms I desperately needed to use. Bruce reminded us that the goal was to get across the country

in a short period of time so he could start his new job
the following week. For that, we needed to get enough
sleep so that we were fresh for the next day.

I followed Bruce to the back of the U-Haul. He
pulled open the storage compartment of the moving
truck, and the giant door hit the top with a loud
thunderous bang. He told Faith and I to grab the two
pillows and sheets then yanked down on the tailgate to
close the truck for the night. I looked at the truck hood
and thought about how I was going to jump on top of it.
I tried to step on the front bumper, but it was dented
and slippery. Plus, I had nothing to help me grip the top
and kept falling backwards.

"Grab my hand and use the front tire to boost
yourself up." Faith then pulled me up with her.

I grabbed the sheet and spread it over the hood
before setting my pillow against the windshield. The
night was cooler than when we left California, but still
muggy. I felt the bugs stick to my sweaty body while I
tried to sleep. The stars were extremely bright, with an
intensity only seen outside city limits.

Bruce stood next to the cab, smoking a joint, and
asked us if we knew any of the constellations. He
chuckled when I told him I didn't even know what the
word meant. He pointed into the sky. The red cherry
from the joint made his fingertip look like it was
glowing in the darkness. He pointed out the Big and
Little Dippers. He told us there were many different
patterns you could only see in the night sky and,

although he didn't know all of them, he did know those two and Orion.

After he was done with the joint, he jumped back in the cab. Faith and I spent the next few hours staring into the night sky, mesmerized with finding other shapes and patterns before we both eventually faded off into a deep sleep.

———

The brightness of the sun coming over the horizon woke me up. It was 5:30. The first rays peaked just over the mountains and filled the valley with pink, yellow, and violet colors as the warm light announced a new day. I wiped the sleep from my eyes and moved Faith's arm to wake her up.

Bruce stretched outside the cab of the truck. "It's time to go. I want to make good time today, so let's head out."

I stepped on the front bumper and jumped to the ground with my pillow in one hand and sheet in the other, ready to put them away for the day.

"How far are we going today?" I asked.

"Probably to Tulsa, then we'll stop again. We'll see how I feel, but I want to get as close to Indiana as possible today."

The rest stop bathroom was only 50 feet from our camping spot, so we grabbed our toothbrush, toothpaste, and a small hand towel to get cleaned up with. We took the cooler from the back of the U-Haul, grabbed chocolate donuts and water for breakfast, then hit the road. I gazed out of the enormous window of the truck as the scenery began to change from boring valleys with far off mountains to red rocks and large boulders.

The mountains felt endless but were an amazing change of pace. Boulders felt like they could fall on us at any minute and there were rocks strewn on the side of the road from rockslides. I watched as we careened up and down twisty mountain roads. Faith and I pointed at cool rock formations and even saw rams standing near the road just below where we were driving, their curvy horns covering most of their heads.

We stopped at a gas station after six hours. All of us needed a pit stop and to stretch our legs before continuing the trip. I really had to use the bathroom. Bruce gave me a homemade box he kept his change in and told me I could play video games inside the gas station while he rested and used the bathroom. I was ecstatic and ran into the small gas station store to jump on the Ms. Pac-Man machine. It was a great break from the monotony and boredom of the trip.

The video game was in the corner near the cashier. The music played as I approached. I grabbed a quarter from the box and set the rest down on the high-top table right next to the game. I hummed the familiar Ms. Pac-Man song and pushed a quarter into the slot, hearing it clank into the bottom of the money catcher. I pressed Player 1 to start the game.

Ms. Pac-Man and I were on fire. The yellow circle, red bow, four ghosts, and challenge of eating all the dots mesmerized me. I lost track of time.

Just as I hit the high score, Bruce walked into the store yelling. "Where in the fuck are you?! I told you to only take 30 minutes."

I scrambled to grab the box of quarters and turned around just in time to see his face contort into an evil snarl, obviously pissed off that he had to come get me.

He gritted his teeth and said in a deep intimidating voice, "I told you to hurry up, but you wanted to be selfish and make us wait." The man at the counter watched as Bruce smacked me in the head and grabbed me by the hair. He pulled me out of the store just as quickly as I'd run in. He shoved me against the side of the U-Haul and my shoulder slammed against the metal frame.

"You just don't fucking listen. You really are fucking stupid." He stared at me and lifted his hand, causing me to flinch and cower.

"Get in the truck and don't say a word," he said to me and Faith.

All three of us jumped back into the cab and sat in awkward silence for the next couple of hours. We passed through Tulsa and stopped for the night at a rest stop just outside the city. The weather was much different than the night before. Light raindrops hit our faces and the truck, causing our sheets to get wet when we put them down on the hood.

I saw red lightning off in the distance. It was hypnotizing. Faith and I propped ourselves up to watch the show. It was something we'd never seen before and a stark contrast to the normal white lightning we were used to. The wind picked up and carried the sounds of howling coyotes in the distance. It seemed like the coyotes were right next to us. I slept with one eye open all night. Bruce finished smoking his joint next to the hood again and told us if it started raining hard to wake him up and we could get in the cab or the back of the truck.

"I think the storm will miss us, but I'm going to bed now because I'm exhausted."

The rain felt good because the night was muggy, but the humidity caused me to sweat profusely. The only reprieve came when the rain dropped a steady drizzle and the wind blew hot air over our bodies. The hood was uncomfortable. I tossed and turned, rolling back and forth. At one point, I almost fell off the side of the truck hood, barely catching myself as one leg hung off the side.

The next day, we continued our journey to Indiana, arriving in the early evening and getting to my uncle's house just in time for dinner. Mom walked out of the bedroom and had stitches running down the middle of her forehead. This startled all of us, especially Faith and me. She'd gotten in a car accident the day after arriving in Indiana. The glass had cut her forehead badly. She told us someone hit her car when she drove through a green light, and she was lucky to be alive. I was thankful that she and Nicole were OK and safe.

I'd grown accustomed to the abuse at the hands of so many different adults in my life. Trading Dad and Gail's abuse for Bruce's didn't bother me. But I was bothered that we moved to an entirely different state. It was a great transition in some regards, as I got to know my mother's family, but also a horrendous one because Bruce easily fell right back into beating us any time he lost his temper.

The ebb and flow of the beatings, combined with times of friendliness, left me confused. The entire culture of Indiana was different, too. Eventually, I became a chameleon of sorts and conformed quickly to our new surroundings.

CHAPTER 7
LOCKED IN THE BASEMENT

We moved to Mulberry, Indiana, a sleepy small town with one main street, two stop lights, and a population of about 1,000 people. This is a place where everyone knows everyone, and all the kids run through the neighborhood playing together.

A train ran through Main Street. The road was bordered by a small city hall, a locally owned grocery store, a pizza place, a jewelry store, and large corn silos at a farm near the end of town. We learned to put nickels on the train tracks just before it came, because it flattened them to the size of a quarter and we could play video games in the grocery store. Faith and I also jumped in the corn silos trying to slide down the corn when they were full. That was incredibly dangerous but also a lot of fun.

The house in Indiana was the nicest place I'd ever lived. It was a Victorian two-story home, light blue with white shutters, and a giant yard with a detached garage. The house had a storm shelter just outside of the back of the house with two giant wooden doors opening from the ground. It led down to a cinder block shelter that we had to use a few times during nearby tornadoes.

That summer, Bruce grabbed a mason jar early one evening as Faith and I tried to catch fireflies in our hands. The amount of glowing bugs lit up the entire yard. Bruce called Faith and I both over to tell us there was a much easier way to catch the firefly's without smashing them in our hands.

Mom sat at the table watching him. She took a drink of her cold beer and cracked another one open for Bruce.

"You have to pop some holes in the top so the fireflies can breathe when you catch them." He handed me the hammer and nail after tapping a few holes in the top and told me to keep going until there were 20 holes. Once I was done putting the holes in the top, he grabbed the bottom of the jar and showed us how we could scoop the fireflies out of the air by pushing them into the jar and quickly tighten the lid so they couldn't fly out.

He helped us catch hundreds of fireflies and then sat the full jar on the table before giving us another one to fill. I was enthralled how the tiny bugs, when put together in a jar, could light up the entire thing like a nightlight in the dark sky, each firefly emitting a light green-yellow hue and captivating my imagination.

Faith and I spent almost every summer night catching fireflies. Nicole was just getting good at walking and waddling around and loved when we'd let her hold the full, glowing jars. But she hated when the bugs would land on her and tried her best to keep up with her brother and sister.

Late in the summer, we had spectacular storms, full of lightning, hail, and intense rain. Mom taught us to run into the storm shelter just in case a tornado was close, reassuring us the shelter would keep us safe. Quite a few times, we'd run down to the shelter in whatever we were wearing. Whether we were in pajamas, a towel from the shower or school clothes, it didn't matter what we had on. This was one time that Mom really made me feel safe because her focus was protecting us, so I never minded being in the shelter when she was there.

———

Later that year, Faith, Nicole, and I celebrated as the first snowfall hit the ground. Blizzard conditions blanketed the entire state for multiple days, dropping two feet of snow.

It took a few days but the weather finally started to break and sunshine broke through, which meant we could go outside. After a few days inside, I was ready to go make snowmen, have snowball fights, and build forts with my friends. It was still five degrees, so Mom told me I had to put on two pairs of socks under my boots, a beanie, thick gloves, and a full body parka. I didn't care what she told me to wear just as long as I got to go play.

Faith helped me get my parka zipped up and we hurried to get the rest of our gear on and go outside. The yelling and laughing of our friends made getting dressed feel like an eternity. I ran to the door and tried to pull it open, but it was stuck. Faith ran over to help me pull it open and we finally got it to budge. It opened with a loud crackling sound as the ice on the rubber peeled off. Snow fell on the welcome mat.

A piercing wind hit me right in my face, instantly reminding me that it was still freezing outside. Once out, I couldn't move well in all my snow gear but was thankful I had a snowsuit on to stay warm. I heard my friends call out for me to hurry because we needed to get our fort ready for the snowball fight.

I ran to the edge of my yard and jumped into the channel that normally caught rainwater. Snowplows pushed the snow in the streets to the side, leaving embankments of snow towering over all of us and creating incredible ready-made fortresses. Kids on both sides of the streets were ready to wage war and built their forts to withstand the force of the imminent snowball attack.

We stacked and pushed the snow up until our side had small steps that allowed us to reach the top of the embankment but still gave us plenty of cover. One of the kids yelled from across the street. "You guys ready?" Little did they know that we were very ready and even had time to make 50 snowballs, giving all five of us ten grenades for the impending attack.

I yelled out, "Fire!" and the game began.

Snowballs flew all over the place. We climbed to the top of our fortresses for better aim before dropping down for cover. We attempted to nail our competition without getting hit. Once you were hit, you were out, so everyone was trying hard to stay in the game.

One of the kids threw a snowball without looking and it hit the passenger window of a passing cop car with a loud *bang*. The officer slammed on his brakes, obviously startled, and slid his car to a stop on the icy road.

All of us panicked as he jumped out of his car and yelled. "Hey, what are all you kids doing?!"

We all stood up at attention. One of the kids, in a squeaky and scared voice, said, "Having a snowball fight, officer."

We were all petrified that he was pissed and we'd all get in trouble. He asked who threw the snowball into his car. I could see my friend's hand rise up from behind the embankment. We apologized to the officer and said that we didn't see him coming down the road. He told us that he remembered his neighborhood snowball fights and started laughing. He told us to be careful and then drove off.

Between snowball fights, sledding, and hot chocolate, winter quickly became one of my favorite seasons.

Soon after, Mom called us to come inside for lunch. Faith and I ran back to the house and smashed through the front door, only slowing our momentum long enough to rip off the multiple layers of snow and sweat soaked clothes. I changed into a clean pair of fleece pajamas Mom had put by the door and ran into the kitchen to eat chicken noodle soup. She set down a mug of hot chocolate with my favorite tiny marshmallows and felt my cheeks with the back of her hand.

"You'd better get all the soup in your belly before you lose any fingers or toes. You're freezing and need to warm up."

I knew she was playing and that I wouldn't lose any body parts, but I played along. "Mom, you saved me from the cold at just the right time."

———

Bruce ended up losing his job later in the year. He told us that we were going to move to Lafayette, about 20 minutes away, because he needed to live where the new work was. The abuse in Mulberry was a lot less than normal because Bruce was happy with his job and making good money. But once he lost his job and we found out we were moving, his entire personality shifted. He became quick tempered and angry.

Little did I know things were about to get much, much worse.

The house in Lafayette was a lot smaller than the one in Mulberry. Gone were the two stories, Victorian charm, and quiet streets. Instead, it was replaced by a very small two-bedroom, single-bathroom home with a fence bordering an alley that opened to the back of other houses. Faith and I could feel that we weren't wanted in the house. We knew that, if we stayed inside, there was a significant possibility we'd get beat, so we usually played outside the entire day.

Most of the time, we'd ride our bikes all over the city, dodging cars, and heading down a giant neighborhood hill as fast as possible without crashing. We did whatever we wanted with no supervision. Catty-corner to our house was a family that had a 120-pound Saint Bernard named Brutus. He was outside on a long chain every day. Brutus was a pretty dog. When he was just lying on the ground, his fluffy white and brown coat could lull you into complacency.

Oftentimes, he would tug and pull on his long chain tied to the oak tree, making every attempt to break free so he could attack you. The bark around the tree rubbed off due to him pulling on the chain. He had a real mean streak and would bark and growl at us as we rode our bikes by him.

Faith and I would repay the gesture by sticking our tongues out, laughing at him, and telling him to shut up. We felt like he couldn't get to us. On occasion he'd get outside and roam around the giant backyard without being tied to the chain, menacing the neighborhood kids or anyone else who passed by.

During the middle of winter, Faith and I were out all day riding our bikes. We started heading home because the streetlights came on and the wind was making both of us really cold. It was sleeting all week and the pavement was slick. The wet puddles turned into patches of ice. The ride home was treacherous. But Faith and I made everything a competition, so we decided to race each other.

Faith said, "Let's race. The loser has to do all the dishes by themselves."

I was fast on my bike and, even though Faith was two years older, I knew I could give her a run for her money. "Bring it. Let's go!" I shouted.

Our rain pants, coats, and socks were soaked from our latest adventure. But we loved bragging rights and hated dishes, so we peddled as fast as we could. Faith was just ahead of me as we neared the alley by the house. I jumped over the curb and tried to get past her and almost slid past the turnoff because it was so slick. Fortunately, I managed to come to a complete stop and regained my balance. Faith paused long enough to laugh at me and make sure I was OK before taking off again.

I planted one foot on the ground and the other on the top pedal to push off, ready to slice through the dirt alley and frozen puddles to win the race. I saw a flash out of the right side of my peripheral vision and knew instantly what it was. Our neighbor's crazy dog, Brutus, was running towards us with a full head of steam. His fur was soaked and his warm breath condensed against the cold, creating an even more ominous view. He had drool dripping from his mouth that sprayed like a sprinkler with every step he took.

I froze, only coming back to life when Faith yelled out, "Oh shit, ride as fast as you can!"

We leaned into the pedals of our bikes as hard as we could, fear propelling us forward. We rode hard towards the house. Brutus ran through his yard, gaining on us and angling towards us like a football player does when going for a tackle. His nailed paws gave him traction and an advantage over our balding BMX tires. I kept turning to look and see how close he was getting. He gained on me quickly, making the last few houses feel like miles.

He snapped at my back tire just as we neared our fence. I jumped off my bike, hoping he would continue to chase it while we ran into the gate. The gate had an icy frozen patch right in front of it that caused Faith, Brutus, and I to slide past it, each of us tumbling over the other. Faith and I landed on the dirt and scrambled to get back up. Brutus landed on his feet, too, but slipped on the ice patch as he stood, giving Faith and I just enough time to get into the gate.

We managed to close and latch the gate just as Brutus slammed his head into it. All three of us breathed heavily. Faith and I stared at each other for a few seconds. Brutus stood there, growling and barking at us.

It felt as if he could knock the gate down or jump over it at any second so I hit Faith on the arm. "Let's get inside the house. Now!" Mom saw the entire thing from the kitchen window and laughed as we ran inside.

She told us, "Well, maybe you two will leave him alone from now on. I've already told you guys to stop messing with him."

I was still breathing heavily from the intense action and laughed as the fear and adrenaline turned into thankfulness that we didn't get eaten alive. I looked over to Faith. "I'm never riding past their house again. We can go all the way around next time."

———

Lafayette was much closer to Moms' parents and brothers' houses. I enjoyed that we were able to see them often. They always treated me well and, even though there was a lot of alcohol, there weren't as many drugs around when we hung out with them. A welcome change.

One of my favorite things to do was drive my Grandpa's John Deer tractor around the acre of front yard he mowed every week. He'd give me his hand so I could reach the steps and I'd jump up to sit on his lap. I'd grip the steering wheel and do my best to keep the lines straight so it looked perfect when I was done. Grandpa would keep one finger on the wheel and provide adjustments, but always made me feel like I was driving.

My grandparent's yard opened to a small pond 100 yards from the back. It was great during the summer, but I really looked forward to winter when the pond froze over. Grandpa told us to stay away from the pond during late winter and early spring. The ice became thinner and, although it looked like we could walk on it, there was a high chance we'd fall in.

It was late winter. Faith and I spent a lot of time around the pond's water edge, walking back and forth to check it out. We were told to check back into the house if we weren't within eyesight, so we'd run back and forth between the pond and the house every so often to confirm we were alive.

On this day, ice still filled the entire pond from edge to edge. The wind whipped across the open area, sending fog into the air while the morning angle of the sun bounced off the ice. It was bright and I felt like I could go blind if I didn't squint.

I grabbed a flat rock and skipped it across the ice, trying to see how far I could throw it before it stopped.

Each time, my rock went a little further, so I continued to throw them in an attempt to break my record. The acoustic dispersion of the sounds reverberating from the ice was incredible. It sounded like exotic birds or a galactic laser blast all coming together to create something I'd never heard before.

After throwing about 20 rocks, I bet Faith that I could walk on the ice. "I bet I can go as far as my rocks did."

"Seriously, Walt, you better not. You could fall in."

I started to step towards the ice, getting ready to throw a rock. Faith grabbed my arm to pull me back. I yanked my arm away and told her that I would throw a heavy rock into the ice and, if it didn't break, then I wouldn't fall through. I was resolute in my confidence that I was correct. The ice would surely be thick enough to be safe.

I swung back and threw the large rock forwards. The rock smashed onto the ice and bounced into the air, chipping the very top layer when it landed. But it didn't go through.

"Ha!" I said, "See? What did I tell ya?" I took a few tentative steps onto the ice.

Faith pleaded with me to get back on shore. But I wanted to prove I wasn't scared. I could make it to my furthest rock. So, I pressed on.

I made it about 20 feet from shore when I heard a loud popping sound. Cracks spider webbed right under my feet. I looked at Faith and back down just fast enough to see the ice give way under me. I fell through the ice. The frigid water felt like ice picks hitting every piece of my skin as my head went under the water.

I reached out just in time to grab the edge, which kept me in the hole instead of under the ice. I couldn't reach the bottom. The cold made it difficult to kick my legs. My boot, jacket, and snow pants filled up with water, weighing me down and making my entire body immediately feel 50 pounds heavier.

Faith let out a loud scream and scrambled to find a long branch to pull me out. She carefully sprawled out on the ice and distributed her weight out so she wouldn't fall in, too.

My muscles seized and grew more tense by the second. But my fear kept me strong enough to grab the stick she was holding out. I used the other hand to pull up on the ice. Faith yanked with all the strength she could muster and tried to pull me back up on the ice.

I kicked my legs feverishly, like a duck in water, but my muscles grew weaker. I managed to get half of my body out of the water just as Faith gave the branch another huge pull. And, finally, I was out! I spread my body over the ice and slowly crawled to the shoreline. I narrowly missed death.

Once we hit the shore, I ran as fast as my body would take me to my grandmother's house. We burst through the door. My lips trembled and my body succumbed to extreme exhaustion as the adrenaline wore off, making it hard for me to strip off my clothes.

Mom told Faith to grab another set of clothes and then helped me get the rest of my wet clothes off. She then covered me with a blanket. I saw Mom's hands trembling as she poured hot water into a cup and made me a mug of hot chocolate.

Once she knew I was OK, her fear turned into anger. She was pissed!

She started yelling at me and Faith. "What the hell were you two doing out there? You could have killed yourselves! We told you to stay away from the ice. I swear you guys don't listen sometimes! Now you know why we don't want you two back there. That part of the area is off limits from now on. You guys better stay away from it for real this time." We took the butt chewing because we knew the rules and didn't follow them.

I was just thankful to be alive.

———

Later, we got home and Mom told me to go to my room because I was in trouble.

"When he gets home, I'm going to let Bruce know you almost died in the pond today."

Faith told me to just stay in the room quietly and maybe Mom wouldn't tell Bruce. I knew I wouldn't be OK if she did. I initially sat in my room, nervous, knowing I was going to get hit and beat because I didn't listen. But, as the hours went on, I almost forgot I was in trouble, especially since Bruce still wasn't home. I played with Lincoln Logs, one of my favorite toys, and became immersed in the scene I was building.

My uncle gave me his kids' two sets of Lincoln Logs. They didn't play with them anymore so I had plenty to spare and could create an entire town. I pulled out my matchbox cars and grabbed my best piece, the Corvette. It was shiny red with a curvy body, big hood, and white-walled black tires that made the perfect centerpiece in the garage I just built.

I put all eight of my cars side by side before laying the foundation for the garage with the logs to ensure I had enough room for all of them. Each log stacked on each other perfectly, fitting into the grooved notches to create a solid structure. I'd left the front of my garage open and took turns driving the cars throughout the town. Each car made different distinct noises.

It was late in the evening. I became lost in thought as I played with the toys but was shaken back into reality when I heard Bruce's truck door slam. I heard his boots on the wooden steps leading up to the front door. It was obvious that he'd been at the bar and was drunk. He slammed the front door, yelling that he was pissed he couldn't find a job because everyone said they weren't hiring until it warmed up in a couple more months.

"On top of that, I have to take care of these two kids who aren't even fucking mine! If it was just you, me, and Nicole we'd be fine. This is fucking bullshit and I'm not going to keep taking care of something that isn't even mine to begin with!"

I heard the clanking of his fork on his plate while he ate dinner and talked to Mom. I hoped and prayed she wouldn't tell him about me falling into the pond earlier in the day. But to no luck. I was surprised as I heard Mom tell him what happened at Grandma's, how she was really scared and pissed I'd be that stupid to go on the pond even though they told us to stay off the ice. I tried my best to be as silent as possible so maybe Bruce would think I was asleep.

I pressed my ear up to the closed door, listening for his reaction and trying to prepare myself for what was next. I heard my heartbeat pick up speed, it's pounding sound penetrating my eardrums and head all at once. I heard Bruce throw his fork. The metal skidded across his plate before hitting the floor.

"That's fucking it! These kids don't want to listen. We'll see if he ever goes out there again when I'm done with him."

His chair slid from the table and his heavy boots started their path to my room, making a loud thud with each individual step he took down the hall.

One...two...three

My heart pounded. I panicked and started looking around but knew I didn't have any place to go.

Four...five...six

I quickly ran back to where I was sitting on the floor to make sure he didn't think I was listening.

Seven...eight...nine

My ears rang as anxiety overtook my thoughts.

Ten.

My body stiffened as he pushed the door open. It banged against the door stopper and bounced back towards him. He moved quickly and stood over the top of me, trying to show his dominance.

He said in a deep voice, "Why in the fuck did you go out on the pond?"

"I don't know why." My voice trembled and my eyes filled with tears.

Everything moved in slow motion. He drew his leg back. I thought he was going to kick me, so I braced myself. Instead, he kicked my Lincoln Log garage into the air. The garage exploded into pieces. Each part flew through the room and hit the wall next to me.

He turned his attention back to me. I held my hand up to block his. He smacked my hand away and slammed his hands down on my head. Bruce grabbed my hair and pulled me to my feet, nearly lifting me off the ground.

"Bullshit. Don't tell me you don't know," he said.

I stuttered and tripped over my words as I tried to reply. "I thought the pond was frozen enough and it would be safe."

"That's right. You're not smart enough to think because you're a fucking idiot, just like your father."

He pulled one hand across his body and backhanded me across the face. The only thing that kept me from being knocked to the ground was the hand holding a fistful of my hair.

He grabbed me by my shirt, pinched into my skin, and pushed me back into the wall before lifting me off the ground to his eye level. My legs dangled helplessly. I turned my head as he put his nose right against mine.

Bruce rumbled in my face, "I hate having you here. You want to hurt yourself, let me show you how to do it the right way."

He turned his body and threw me across the room. My back hit the glass-framed picture, knocking all the breath out of me. I immediately felt pain shoot through my head as it bounced off the glass. My eye was shut from the first smack and now my vision blurred.

My whole body hurt. My head throbbed in pain. My eye swelled shut. And now my back felt bruised from hitting the edge of the picture frame. I slid down the wall and felt shards of glass fall on top of my head. I brushed my hand over my hair and saw blood from the cut on my head. I grimaced because it was tender. I also felt pieces of glass in the rest of my hair, so I shook my head back and forth trying to get it out. My ears rang so bad that shaking my head was even more dizzying.

I looked up towards Bruce, trying not to make eye contact but not really knowing what was next. I was scared, fearful he was going to kill me, and felt like I might bleed to death from my head wound.

My eight-year-old imagination ran wild in that moment and a panic attack set in. I wanted to run, but there was nowhere to go. I fell to my side from the dizziness and just wanted to lie on the floor. His boots got closer and he took two steps towards me. I covered my face with my hands, trying to protect myself. I didn't want to look back at his face, but I could hear him breathing heavily now. He reared his leg back and kicked me in my thigh.

"Get the fuck up. I'm going to show your sorry ass what happens when you don't listen and what your punishment is going to be for as long as you live here."

He grabbed me by the arm. His hand wrung it tight like a starving python that just captured its first meal in months, not willing to let go, no matter what I did. He pushed me in front of him. My knees buckled, but he was determined to move me in the direction he wanted. I didn't know where we were going. I felt sick to my stomach.

He stopped at the basement door right next to the kitchen and swung the door open. I understood now he was about to throw me into the basement and into the dark. I leaned back ready to fight for my life.

I hated the basement; it was dark, damp, and scary. Bruce kept a werewolf Halloween mask that he would use to scare me with down there. Whenever I was near it, I felt like it came alive, waiting and ready to kill me. I didn't feel the pain in my body anymore. The fear came over me like a tsunami. My flight or fight response was in full intensity. I tried to push back against him. The darkness seemed so black. Black like a coffin.

Bruce shook me, causing my leg and hand to release the door jam.

I fought as hard as I could and screamed over and over. "No! Please don't put me down there!" But it fell on deaf ears.

He reared back and smacked my leg so hard that it welted my thigh. The pain defeated me. It hurt so terribly. I stopped resisting.

Bruce pushed me into the basement. I fell over the first few steps. I scraped my knees and barely caught myself from falling down to the bottom. He stood at the top of the stairs and said I'd be staying there until he felt like letting me out. He tapped on the light switch and said he would hurt me even worse if I touched it. Bruce stared at me for a few seconds then slammed the door shut, telling me that I better get used to being down there.

I shakily wobbled up from my knees and got to my feet. I was exhausted from the entire day and scared as hell. I grabbed the handle and tried to turn it. It was locked from the outside. Panic set in because I knew at that exact moment that I was trapped and there was no way out. I banged with both hands on the door and began screaming.

My voice reverberated against the hollow door panels and caught my screams as I pleaded. "Please let me out! Please let me out. Please let me out."

I grimly realized after a few minutes that nobody was coming to let me out. I was going to need to find a way to survive. The silence was deafening once I stopped screaming. I knew at that moment that I was stuck down there by myself.

I sat on the top stair, petrified to go down to the bottom of the basement, knowing the werewolf Halloween mask was down there. It came alive when I was in the dark. I could hear the *click, click, click* of the werewolf's nails tapping on the floor, waiting for me at the bottom so it could eat me alive.

I made myself as small as I could and curled into a ball. I gripped my knees to my chest and wrapped my arms so tightly around them nothing could break through. I closed my eyes, trying to imagine I was in another place, another time. Anywhere but here.

Somehow, over time, I found peace in the mind-numbing terror every time he threw me into the basement. But I knew I couldn't hold onto my sanity and endure the tortuous abuse for much longer. Something had to change!

A few months later, Mom told Faith and I that we were going to live with Dad again in San Diego. We'd be flying there the following week. She'd realized the abuse and torture Bruce was putting me through was too much, and she needed to get Faith and me out of there before he killed us. Mom told us she was leaving Bruce.

I didn't know what to really think, but I knew I was glad to be moving back with Dad. I didn't think I could survive the abuse Bruce was putting me through any longer.

CHAPTER 8
OCEAN BEACH

The plane landed on the tarmac with a loud thud. The four engines of the 747 roared and pulled me forward in my seat. The plane slowed from hundreds of miles an hour to incrementally taxiing down the runway, making its way to the gate—and my new life.

The captain's voice came over the loudspeaker. "Welcome to San Diego. You can unbuckle your seatbelt. Flight attendants make the cabin ready for arrival."

I breathed a sigh of relief knowing I made it out of the purgatory in Indiana. Even though Dad hit us, at this moment it was better than staying with Bruce. I was ecstatic I wouldn't have to see Bruce again but sad that I left my mom and Nicole. At the same time, I was apprehensive about living with my dad, and thankful Faith and I stayed together.

The stewardess was super friendly as she made her way over to Faith and me to ask us to stay seated while the rest of the plane disembarked. Faith and I watched each passenger, one by one, struggle to get their carry-on baggage out of the overhead compartment and make their way out of the plane.

Everyone seemed in a hurry. Some people were smiling. Some looked serious. Some looked inpatient. I pondered what they were thinking and where they were going. Do they have happy families they are seeing? Are any of them going to live with someone they don't want to? Are their families waiting for them, too? I stared in their direction in hopes that by some sort of miracle I might get to go with one of the smiling people and start a new life with them.

While we waited, Faith turned to me and said, "I'm so happy to finally be out of Indiana. I sure hope Dad will be different this time, especially since he's not with Gail anymore."

I was nervous, exhausted, and filled with trepidation. I was tired of being abused by every adult we lived with. It was taking its toll on my mentality, spirit, and soul. I didn't want to get hit or thrown in basements anymore—nothing more, nothing less. I wondered if Dad would even want us this time or if he'd drop me off on Mom's doorstep when he grew tired of us like he did before.

I sighed as the stewardess told us to follow her. I imagined I was in an alternative life where things were different and not filled with turmoil and pain. The lump in my throat continued to grow as Faith and I made our way up the blue carpeted hallway. I felt her hand squeeze mine just a little tighter. Her nervousness was just as high as mine, but she tried to keep a brave façade for me.

Dad greeted us with a huge grin at the gate and thanked the stewardess for taking care of us. I felt a bit thrown off because I barely remember him being happy. I stood there staring at him for a minute and contemplated my next thought.

"C'mon over here, Junior. I'm so excited to see both of you guys." He seemed so joyful and the elation emanating from him made me feel safe, loved, and, for the first time in a long time, hopeful. I finally ran up to him, praying the alternate reality I dreamt up might actually be true.

Dad gave me a hug. "How old are you? Are you 25 yet?" He ruffled the hair on the top of my head.

I instinctively flinched and immediately had flashbacks of Bruce yanking my hair and dragging me towards the basement. I didn't realize it at the moment, but Dad was trying to give me a loving touch. I didn't recognize it because in the almost nine years I was alive those loving touches were so few and far between. The effects from being thrown in the basement, compiled with the years of physical, mental, and emotional abuse created an alternative reality of what love actually looked like.

Dad pursed his lips in surprise and tilted his head a little to the right. He told me life will be different this time and we're going to have a blast together so I didn't need to worry anymore. He put his hand on my shoulder and smiled as he kneeled down to my eye level.

"C'mon, if you're not 25, then you must be at least 15 by now, right?"

His softness disarmed me, and I laughed. I smiled and told him he knew I was almost nine and he was trying to be funny. Dad laughed, grinned with his sly smile, and told me he did really know, he just wanted to see if I was paying attention.

Dad told Faith and me, "I've waited for a long time to live together again and, with Gail not living with us, it will be a lot calmer."

I prayed he was right and that we would have fun, but I still felt slightly apprehensive, which fueled my nervousness. We followed Dad down to the luggage area and waited until a large buzzer sounded. The belt started to move and we watched each bags drop. Faith told Dad our suitcase was blue and had both our names on it. I was watching and ran over to the bag when I saw it onto the conveyor.

I tried to pull it off and onto the floor but the bag was pretty heavy. A gentleman standing close by saw me struggling and pushed the back end of the suitcase towards the edge so I can wrangle it to the floor.

I looked over at Dad. "See? I got it!"

Dad grabbed my bicep. "Wow, Junior, you're really strong."

I had a smile of pride from ear to ear as I pulled the suitcase through the airport and towards the car.

Once we loaded our luggage, I told dad I was really hungry and wanted to get something to eat. He said we could go to McDonalds on the way home. I was excited because happy meals always had toys, and we didn't have very many anymore. He told us about how cool his duplex is. He said it was across the street from the beach and, even though it was small, we'd be OK until he could find something bigger.

I could tell he was really excited because, out of nowhere, he started belting out the lyrics to his favorite song by The Mamas and the Papas playing on the radio.

He bellowed out the lyrics in a deep voice, bobbing his head up and down. Dad looked over at Faith in the front seat and asked if she'd heard the song before. We'd both heard the song, but neither of us actually knew the words. What I did know was, for the first time in a long time, we were around positive energy. Dad's happiness made both of us optimistic that our life was going to have a fresh start.

———

We parked in front of the duplexes. I asked excitedly, "Is our place the one with the big window right here in the front because it looks incredible?"

"Unfortunately, ours is in the back and doesn't have a big window. But it has a nice patio."

I didn't really care which one ours was. I was just excited to see it. He grabbed our suitcase and walked us down the dark narrow hallway to the second unit. He slid the key in the door and opened it all the way.

"Go ahead, go inside kids. This is your home now."

Faith walked in first and turned to me to say, "This is really nice!" before moving in so I could see, too.

The duplex was cozy. The front door opened right into the living room. There was a couch on the wall to the left and a blue fabric recliner centered on the TV. Dad had a red light in the lamp that made the room darker. He headed to the kitchen to turn on a light so we could see better. The kitchen was small enough for one person to be in there at once, and there was a small table with two chairs to eat on.

"Come to your bedroom and check it out. I got you guys bunk beds to share and I'll be sleeping on the couch. My friend and I built those beds just yesterday for both of you."

Faith and I both said thank you at the same time.

Dad pointed to the bathroom. "The bathroom is a little tight and there's only one, but we'll make do for now."

He set our luggage down in the bedroom and told us that we could unpack tomorrow night. "For now, we're going to eat McDonald's, watch a movie, and cook this delicious popcorn." He shook the popcorn bag on the counter.

Dad carried on. "Just wait until you two get to see how close the beach is. We're going to head over there tomorrow, and I'll show you around your new town."

I never lived so close to the beach. Even though we lived in San Diego before, we never really went, so I was a bit dumbfounded.

I asked Dad if he meant the beach with the ocean and waves.

He laughed. "That's the exact beach I'm talking about, son. I can't wait to take you guys."

I was famished. The cheeseburgers, fries, and soda tasted really good. Even though the house was tiny it felt like a home already. I asked where Patrick was because I expected to see him at the house. Dad told me he was still living with Gail.

We finished dinner and Dad said it was time to start the popcorn so we can watch the movie. He began singing a song and called me into the kitchen.

"Grab that big bowl under the counter and three Pepsi's from the fridge for us, son." Dad said.

I could smell the salt and butter as he dumped three bags of popcorn into a huge red plastic bowl. I grabbed our drinks and headed into the living room. He patted the cushion and told us to jump onto the couch with him. He put his arms around Faith and I and gave us a kiss on the top of our heads.

"You guys are in for a treat." He carried on as he grabbed the remote and pressed play. The opening scene of *Top Gun* started. I leaned in to watch the fighter jets scream across the screen.

———

The next day, we went to the beach and I could hardly contain my joy. Dad reminded us that there were a lot of vagrants at the beach and, for our safety, to stay within eyesight while we're at the oceanfront. It was an extremely short walk to the beach. On the way, he pointed out a grassy area just across the street from the house. He told me that he would teach me how to play his favorite sport, baseball.

We continued along a sidewalk and parking lot before coming to a barrier formed by rocks jutting out into the ocean. I was super inquisitive about the rock barrier, Dad told me all about why they built them and how it separated the people side of the beach from the side you can bring dogs on. We stopped between both sides to watch the dogs from just in front of the lifeguard tower.

Dad leaned down next to me and pointed out the dogs racing into the water in hot pursuit of their tennis balls. Their paws hit the surf at full speed and they jumped into oncoming waves, creating a spray that flew into the air. I finally told Dad I was ready to go into the water, so we headed over to his favorite spot.

We walked down towards the ocean and set out a sheet to lie on. Dad told us to unpack the chairs right behind the sheet so we could keep our belongings in front of us. The chairs were hard to open as they were sandy and rusty from the salty air. Each of the chairs had blue and red webbing cut in a crisscross pattern and sat just above the ground, placing you eye level with the waves. I loved this.

Dad told us to put on sunblock before we went in the water. The beach sun was famous for quickly giving sunburns. He rubbed the sunblock on my back as I danced back and forth, jumping up and down like a jackrabbit until he finally tapped my back and said I could go.

The day was slightly overcast. The midday sun pushed against the fog like two gladiators wrestling for position over all the people below. The blue lifeguard towers were sprinkled throughout the sandy beach. They stood tall and were filled with tanned and fit women and men looking through binoculars at the crowd, ready to save a wayward swimmer at any moment.

I sprinted into the ocean as fast as my body would take me. The cold Pacific waters shocked me momentarily as the spray hit my legs. My momentum carried me into an oncoming wave and I jumped into it before being thrown right back on my butt. I got back up and ran towards the next wave, this time jumping through it and coming out the other side like I watched Faith do. The sea foam sprayed my face and kelp tried to grab at my legs, making it hard to stand. But I was in heaven. I threw my hands forward, splashing the water, and pushed my sandy blond hair away from my face. I stared out into the abyss. This was absolute paradise.

Faith ran up and jumped on my back. We both crashed into the water, laughing, literally having one of the best days of our young lives. Like most kids looking for their parents' approval, we looked back at Dad to see him smiling and waving.

He hollered out, "Don't go in the water too far and stay where you can reach!"

Faith and I chimed back in unison, "OK! We will be careful!"

We ran and jumped in the waves for a couple of hours, coming back to shore only to drink water when we were thirsty. Dad finally called us back in and said it was time to head to the house and get something to eat before we starved to death.

He handed me four empty Bud Light cans and told me to hurry and throw them in the trashcan on the other side of the lifeguard station. We began walking back to the house, but my shorts were still full of sand and my legs chafed as the salt dried on them. I felt uncomfortable, sticky, and tired as we came around the corner of the duplex.

The impact of jumping in the waves all day in the heat finally caught up to me. Dad told us to go around the back of the house to hose ourselves off. He said to make sure we got all of the sand off before we came inside, and he'd make some lunch.

Faith and I hosed each other off, making sure we got every speck of sand from our bathing suits and bodies. It felt amazing to get the sand and sticky salt cleaned off. We sat on the small concrete pad in the sun out back while Dad handed us some sandwiches and Doritos to eat. He pulled up a chair next to us and talked about how great the day was.

"You guys both need to shower before bed. Tomorrow is your first day in your new school."

We'd moved in the middle of the school year, so I knew we'd have to start a new school soon. But I didn't have much excitement left anymore for new school adventures. The reality that I'd need to make new friends all over again felt daunting. The only thing that gave me peace was knowing Faith would be a fifth grader, ruling the school and making sure I was OK in my third grade class.

———

The next day, the teacher called me up to the front of the class and introduced me. She said I was from Indiana and the kids should all welcome me with open arms. Most of the kids were nice, but I saw a few snickering in the back and pointing at me.

During recess, a couple of mean-spirited kids started making fun of me. They called me a skeleton because I was so skinny and made fun of the holes in my jeans and called me poor. The three kids continued to tease the way I looked, pointing out my pudgy nose and the large gap between my teeth. I was full of rage and wanted to hurt them and myself.

I hated this school, class, town, and myself. I wanted to run away and scream, cry out loud because I had to start all over again. Dad was waiting for us when we got home. He had just gotten home from work and was excited to see how the day went.

I didn't really know what to say. "It was fine. There were both nice and mean kids at the school."

He didn't notice the tears in my eyes as I left the room. But, as I closed my bedroom door, I heard him saying that I should give it a few weeks before passing final judgment on the school.

He came into my room after a little while. "You want to know something cool?"

I said yes because anything at that point was better than the day I just had.

I followed him out to the living room. He popped *Top Gun* back in and fast forwarded to scenes at the Navy base in Point Loma.

"I deliver classified mail to buildings on the base where these scenes were filmed. I want to take you on my route soon so you can see just where they happened in real life."

"That's awesome. I can't wait to check it out over the weekend. I really want to go," I said.

He grabbed a bag from next to the couch. "I have a present for you. Something to make your day better."

"What present?" I smiled with excitement. We didn't get many presents, so the thought of receiving one took the pain from a horrible first day of school away.

Dad pulled out a brand-new baseball glove and threw it towards me. I was pumped to put it to use immediately. The smell of the brand-new leather and light tan color was perfect.

"We need to put a ball in the pocket of the glove, use oil to moisturize the leather, and wrap it closed with a shoestring to break it in before using it. It's a secret trick all the pros use to make sure the glove opens and closes easily."

Dad grabbed a baseball and tossed it to me. "I'm going to make you an all-star so you can play for the San Diego Padres one day."

I was so happy and excited to learn how to play baseball from Dad that I blurted out, "Can we start right now?" even though it was dark outside.

"I have something even better since it's getting dark outside already. Let's order some pizza and watch the Padres game together tonight. I can give you some pointers during the game."

I couldn't wait to learn how to play baseball and make him proud, so I sat and watched the entire game without getting up. Just before the game started, he took out an MLB official scoring book and told me to come sit next to him.

The book looked fancy and had a baseball diamond on the cover. Dad was extremely meticulous when he was writing or keeping stats on anything. He told me it's what the MLB uses to officially keep stats during the games and, by understanding the nuances of the game, it will make me a lot better than the other kids. We sat there keeping score for three hours as he described in detail all the finer points of baseball.

Dad took me over to the grassy area next to the beach for the next few months to prepare me for the upcoming baseball season. Dad was an accomplished baseball player when he was younger. He taught me all the tips and tricks he knew about batting, fielding, and throwing. Faith joined along, too, but she wasn't as nearly into baseball as me. Instead, she preferred basketball because she was tall. The joy I had from learning sports from Dad was insatiable and I couldn't get enough of it. I wanted to practice every day because it meant I could have time with him.

This was one of the happiest and toughest times of my childhood. On one hand, I struggled to make friends at school and endured relentless bullying because we were so poor. On the other hand, it was the happiest I'd ever seen Dad and the most consistent safe environment I'd ever had. Eventually, through becoming good at baseball, I made more friends. The kids who bullied me found a new respect for me because one of them played on my team and I was extremely good.

Little did we know the honeymoon phase of living with Dad was about to come to an end a few months later.

Dad came home and said he was laid off from his job. He told Faith and I that he was going on disability due to reinjuring an old back problem he got in the Army lifting tank rounds. Dad relapsed into abusing prescription pills and his drinking became extremely heavy. This led to a slippery slope of hunger, abuse, and darkness that engulfed the entire one-bedroom house in Ocean Beach.

CHAPTER 9
THE DARKNESS RETURNS

Money became tight and food was scarce. Many days, Faith and I went without eating unless we went to school and ate the free lunch, which wasn't an option during summer break. We resorted to rationing peanut butter, eating it straight off a spoon for dinner and trying to make it last until my dad got his disability check on the first of the month.

One night, the only thing in the house to eat were frozen lima beans that had been sitting in the freezer for months. I didn't want to eat those, so I looked in the kitchen one last time. The cupboards were bare, and we'd eaten the last of the peanut butter a couple of days before. The only other items in the house to eat besides the lima beans were two beers. I was starving and heard my stomach rumbling. With no other options, and my hunger pains growing, I decided to cook the lima beans. I boiled a pot of water, dumped in the freezer-burnt clumps, and attempted to follow the directions on the package.

I felt angry and pissed off as I stood over the boiling water. I wondered where Dad was, and if he got himself something to eat. I knew he was at the bar down the street getting drunk and didn't care if we ate or not. The feelings of love, hope, and a new, improved Dad faded quickly as his drinking increased. Returned was the dad that haunted my dreams from time to time, the one who beat us incessantly when he and Gail were together, the dad who left us on the curb at Mom's house without even a hug goodbye or "I love you."

Faith and I became Dad's servants, required to do everything domesticated in the house. When we had food, we cooked for Dad and served his meals on a plate while he sat in his recliner. Faith and I would walk a mile to Safeway to buy food with food stamps so he could eat what he wanted at the beginning of every month. Once he spent all of his disability money on alcohol and cigarettes, he'd have us walk to multiple stores and buy $.05 candy with the food stamps until we gathered enough change that he could go drinking or buy more beer.

Faith and I also did all of the laundry at Wonderland Coin and Laundry, about three blocks from the house. It was a locally owned place, its red painted facade peeling, long weathered by the salty breeze of the ocean. It's twenty washers and dryers were being used every single time we showed up, requiring us to wait for a turn.

Adults would stare at Faith and I as we used all of our strength to pull, drag, and carry the laundry to the laundromat and back home in pillowcases, doing our best to keep it clean and get it home without dumping it onto the ground.

Dad sent me to the Pat's Liquor store two blocks from the house daily to fetch cigarettes and beer when he wasn't at the bar. Pat's Liquor had a giant neon sign in the front with "Liquor" in large horizontal letters and "Pat's" in cursive over the top of the sign. It was small with only the capacity to hold maybe five to six customers at once, but I was always welcomed when I came through the door.

Pat was a nice and friendly man who always had a smile on his face. He gave me quarters from the cash register so I could play the 10-yard fight football video game standing in the corner. He even allowed me to take a small bag of chips for free before I left. He always made my trip to the store worth the walk.

Dad was in a lot of pain from his injury. His aggravation and temper grew considerably in a short period of time. His mood shifted the entire dynamic of our home and left us walking on eggshells every day, unsure if we'd get abused at any moment. He would have Faith and I constantly bring his "Cod's and Rob's," his Codeine and Robaxin narcotic pills for pain and muscle relaxation. I knew if I didn't scurry through the house quickly enough, I'd get smacked. So, I'd spring to action, bringing him three of each anytime he said to.

His drinking was also at an all-time high and his anger spilled over when he mixed the pills and beer.

"Bring me a fucking beer, boy," he'd say grumpily throughout the day.

I could tell he hated me and could see him staring when I'd grab his beer, sometimes noticing a considerable shift in his entire demeanor.

One time he looked at me and said, "You know what, Junior? Your mom doesn't love you and she dumped you fucking kids off in my lap. I didn't even want you. My life was great before you and your sister got here."

I froze and knew anything I said would be wrong in the moment, but inside I was devastated and crying out. I'd look down at my shoes, trying not to make direct eye contact because I knew what he was capable of and didn't want to trigger him. These types of mood swings were extreme and a commonality in our house.

For example, just a few hours earlier in the same day, he was yelling my name as I rounded first and slid into second base.

He was in the stands of my baseball game hollering out after my first hit. "Way to go, Junior!! That's my boy right there."

I was quickly becoming one of the best baseball players in San Diego and felt the pride beam from him during those moments at the game. It was the only thing bonding the two of us and the only time I received anything positive from him. Games seemed like they were the only time we saw him smile, the darkness surrounding him dominated his thoughts and actions. He became unrecognizable and a totally different person.

———

I heard Dad fumbling with his keys at the front door. He swung the door open so hard that it slammed against our entertainment center. He caught himself on the couch as he stumbled inside. The smell of cigarettes and alcohol permeated from every pore in his body. We were hungry because there was no food in the house, and I was tired of starving all the time. I asked him in a snarky voice if we were going to get any dinner and it threw him into a rage.

While he yelled, he lost his balance and fell onto the couch. He swayed back and forth, not saying a word, just sitting there and staring at me. I hurt inside and was beginning to really hate him. I had deep feelings of anger hiding behind my fear, but still present in the way I talked to him that night. I walked back towards my room with Faith to escape his wrath and watched as he fell out of the couch when he tried to get his boots off.

He called out for me, "Junior, get your ass back out here. I didn't say I was done with you."

I came back into the living room. "What?" My anger overflowed out of me.

"Pull my boots off."

I thought of leaving him there on the floor. But, even though I was really angry, I felt bad for him.

I slid the first boot off easily but couldn't get the second boot off because he kept moving his foot. I pulled on it with all my might and tried to shake the boot loose by moving it back and forth.

He yelled for me to let go and said in a slurred voice, "You're fucking weak, just like your mother."

He turned and looked at Faith, telling her, "You, too, you stupid bitch. You look just like your mother."

I didn't know what he was about to do, but I could see the anger and hate growing on his face. I let go of the boot and his foot hit the floor, jarring him forward. He reacted by kicking me in my chest. The heavy heel of his brown boot left a dirt mark on my shirt from my chest to my stomach and knocked me onto the ground. He gave me an evil glare and his bottom jaw jutted out further than the top. He furrowed his eyebrows in anger, and his voice took on an entirely different tone.

"You motherfucker."

Dad reminded me of the hateful way Bruce stared at us. At that moment, my own father turned into a monster just like Bruce. I hated them both and just wanted to run. Instead, I froze in fear because I didn't have any place to go. It was terrifying.

Faith reacted and yelled out, "Why did you kick him?"

Dad immediately became unhinged. I heard a clanking sound as Dad stood up and unbuckled his belt and ripped it off all in one movement.

He folded it over to make a snapping sound, which he'd do to intimidate us, and started yelling, "You stupid motherfuckers! Who in the fuck do you think you are?"

Dad swung the belt wildly and with reckless abandon until we had welts on our hands, arms, legs, and faces. When he exhausted himself and finished hitting us, he fell back onto the couch.

The tortuous abuse seemed to get worse every day. Dad would leave the house all day, only coming back once he was drunk. Sometimes he'd pass right out and sometimes he'd take out his anger on the two of us. The small duplex quickly became like a prison and we were trapped inside.

Dad was gone during the day so much that Faith and I were left to fend for ourselves and had the run of Ocean Beach. We took full advantage of getting away from the house at every opportunity and explored the entire city and coastline, walking miles away from the house every day. There are so many examples of how we'd put ourselves in danger while exploring. Sometimes it was the ocean and sometimes it was a vagrant trying to lure us in the bathroom. Faith and I were inseparable and everyday became an adventure together.

Faith and I walked up to the rock barrier jutting out about 50 yards into the ocean, between the dog beach and normal beach. Even though we'd been in this location a few times before we saw what looked like a tunnel for the first time.

"Climb down there, Faith," I said as we scampered over the rocks towards the hole just big enough for two skinny kids to slide down.

"OK. Let me check it out," she said as she slid down the rock.

Faith disappeared for a few seconds before returning. "There is a full tunnel down here. It's big enough for both of us."

It sounded fun so I slid down the rock and joined her. The rocks inside were propped up on each other to prevent shore erosion. To us, this became our own special cave. It had just enough space for us to weave back and forth through the maze of rocks on the inside. We joked that, if we looked hard enough, there might be a pirate's treasure down there.

Faith said, "If we find some treasure, we'll run away and start a new life away from everyone else."

The rocks got more slippery as we made our way towards the front of the barrier. The tide got our feet wet and the occasional spray from a bigger wave hit us in the face like rain as it passed through the maze of rocks.

With water all the way up to our knees, we peered out the front of the barrier between a crack in two rocks just in time to see a giant wave crash over the entire thing. The force of the water knocked us down and took our breath away. Our tunnel immediately filled with water. We panicked as multiple waves surged into our small space, pulling and pushing us against the rocks. Right when I thought we were going to drown, the water receded and we ran because we knew another set of waves was barreling towards us.

"Run!" We both yelled out as we moved like world class rock climbers through the boulders, making our way back to the spot we entered.

"Don't look back!" I yelled as we heard the loud thundering impact of another wave hitting the rocks behind us.

I felt the water hit our feet as it continued to surge in. We scrambled out of the rocks and back to safety just in time. Faith and I ran back onto the beach and laughed hysterically as soon as our feet touched the warm sand, each of us knowing we were lucky to be alive.

The freedom of being out of the house and running all over Ocean Beach was cathartic in a way only the truly oppressed can feel. Day over day, we'd hit the door after my Dad left for the bar. Even once the school year started, we'd run all over town doing the dangerous things kids do when unsupervised because, most nights, Dad wouldn't come home until sometime after dark.

That winter, the ocean was in a frenzied state as a storm surge pushed in. The waves crashed over the top of the pier, leaving a spray of salty water that exploded hundreds of feet in the air.

Faith and I ventured down to the Ocean Beach downtown area. We walked past the world-famous Hodads restaurant. I loved how they hung surfboards, cars, and license plates on the walls. We continued to walk past a small ice cream shop. Whenever we passed the ice cream shop, we'd stop to look through the windows in hopes of having money to buy some strawberry or cookie dough ice cream one day.

We continued walking towards the beach, mesmerized by the power of the ocean. The waves hit the concrete retaining wall with a thunderous roar that sounded like 10,000 elephants breaking through a barrier. We turned to see a man stretched out and passed out on the sidewalk. His hair was matted, his clothes dirty and tattered. He had a belt tied around his arm and a heroin needle on the ground right next to him. I thought he was dead and watched as people walked around him like he wasn't even there.

There were others dressed the same way and I noticed many seemed to be talking to themselves. Faith and I walked past another small group smoking weed in the parking lot. I could tell it was weed by the familiar pungent stinky skunk smell. People stared at us as we walked by because we were only nine and eleven. Nobody said anything until one of the people in the group smoking weed yelled out, "You kids need to stay away from the pier!" His booming voice startled me and both of us took off in a sprint to get as far away as possible.

We finally made it to the pier and set our sights on a steep slope full of damp, ocean-sprayed pigeon point shrubs just under the bottom of the pier. The pier was closed, but Faith and I wanted to get a closeup view of the ocean's power. The magnetic pull of the waves became undeniable. We started our steep ascent up the 40-foot hill running from the bottom of the pier to the retaining wall. The shrubs were slippery from the ocean spray coming off the retaining wall, but after about five minutes we made it to the top unscathed.

We sat and watched the power of God unfold in front of us as the ocean continued to pummel the retaining wall below. Faith and I didn't say much. We were mesmerized by the power in the moment. I started to wonder what would happen if I fell in, and if I would get swept away to a better life far away from here. Anything seemed better than going back to our purgatory and hell of a home. I was brought back to reality when Faith hit me on my arm and pointed towards the sidewalk.

We saw a lifeguard running from the giant headquarters building. He was waving his arms wildly and mouthing something we couldn't understand because of the deafening sound of the ocean below. I wasn't even sure if he was talking to us until he ran up the steps of the pier and got within a few feet from where Faith and I were sitting below on the shrubs.

"What the hell are you kids doing? You're going to get killed out here!"

While he spoke, a large wave crashed over the retaining wall and onto the bottom of the slope we sat on. The ground shook beneath my feet and the spray soaked all my clothes. The water crested just twenty feet below us before receding back down the hill.

He urgently reached his hand out. "Damn it! Both of you guys get over here before you're swept away and drowned."

We carefully got up from our seats and grabbed his hand while he pulled us up and over the barrier and back into safety. He asked where our parents were and we told him in the restaurant right down the street. We knew if we said we were alone, he would call the cops or CPS. So, when he turned his head back towards the lifeguard headquarters, we took off running.

We were soaked from head to toe, our hair dripping down our backs, shoes squeaking with every step. I knew I definitely didn't want them to call Dad and tell him we were below the pier. We ran as fast as we could all the way home and never looked back. Even though what we were doing was extremely dangerous, it didn't feel like it during those moments. In spite of being around vagrants, drugs, and the pounding ocean waves, being together always made Faith and I feel safer.

———

As the months passed, the abuse escalated and became an almost everyday occurrence. Punches, smacks, pulled hair, kicks, belts, name calling, and neglect became the norm. You could see the darkness flowing out of my dad like a thick cloud, the pain in his eyes intensely staring back at us as he got lost in his own suffering. I only learned later that he had been molested by another man when he was a teenager, which likely spurred him to be this way. Dad's uncontrolled rage emanated from his face as he sauntered around, his lips contorting and his voice changing like he was possessed, especially when he was drunk.

Faith started talking to me about a plan to escape; she couldn't take the abuse anymore and wanted to hurt herself.

She told me one day that Dad had molested her. "I have to get the fuck out of here before I kill him or myself."

I felt terrible for her because I could see the pain in her eyes and, even though I knew I couldn't, I wished I could take it away. I wanted to go with her but felt terrified Dad would find out our plan and kill us both. It took a few weeks, but Faith figured out how to call

Mom from a payphone. The two of them devised a plan to get us out of the house almost immediately.

Faith was in sixth grade now. Since her middle school had lockers, she snuck outfits out of the house everyday over the next week and left them there. She layered clothes on her body and stuck some in her book bag so she wouldn't go to Mom's without anything. Faith was stealthy and made it seem like everything was normal, fooling Dad who was home sitting on the couch when we left in the morning.

Then the day came for her to leave. We left the house and made our way towards the school. I told Faith that I was petrified Dad was watching and secretly knew what we were doing. Faith wanted to make sure he wasn't, so we took a few side streets to ensure we weren't being tailed before we sprinted towards our rendezvous point. I was quiet on the walk, but Faith talked a lot, begging me to leave with her.

She kept telling me, "I don't want to leave you with Dad by yourself, but I need to get the hell out of here. Please come with me."

We ended up across the street from the Jack in the Box where Mom was supposed to meet us and heard a lady yell out, "Hey, little kids."

It startled both of us. Faith yelled back at the lady, "Go fuck yourself, lady."

Mom yelled back to us, "It's me, Mom."

Her hair was really short. We didn't recognize her until she yelled at us. We both breathed a sigh of relief, but I was still paranoid Dad would jump out of the bushes at any moment. Faith was so thankful she'd made it to Mom safely and was about to leave forever. I had a pit in my stomach. I didn't want to get separated from my sister and best friend.

Mom told us she moved back to Hemet and was staying with a friend. "We need to go, kids. I don't feel comfortable knowing your dad could walk up any minute."

I told Mom that I wasn't going. "I don't want to be around Bruce again."

"I'm not with Bruce anymore, honey. This time things are different."

I wanted to go with Faith so badly but, no matter how much I wanted to, the fear of knowing Dad could take us back dominated my thoughts. I felt like he'd kill me for being a traitor and leaving with Mom.

Faith gave me a long hug. One of those hugs when you know you may never see someone again. We both started crying because we knew this was it.

With tears in her eyes, Faith pleaded with me one last time to come. "Please, Walt, please come with me, brother. I don't want Dad to hurt you anymore and we'll be together."

"I just can't go, sis. I can't do it."

I didn't have the courage Faith had in the moment to run away. The soul-crushing fear I felt crippled my capability to leave. The multiple times we'd been kidnapped or dropped with each parent negated any trust I had of being safe if I went with Mom. I also didn't believe Bruce wouldn't be in the picture. I could take the physical abuse and narcissism, but I knew my mind couldn't take being thrown in a basement again.

I finally hugged them both goodbye. Mom and Faith got into their car and left. I stood in the parking lot, watching their car disappear in the distance as they drove away. I felt frozen in time and my heart was broken in a million pieces. I felt the deepest sense of loneliness I'd ever felt as I stood there contemplating the decision I'd just made and feeling instant regret.

A car honked its horn at me because I was standing in the middle of the parking lot and startled me out of the surreal moment. I snapped back into the reality of the day and realized I needed to get to school before I was late for class. Dad would beat me if I wasn't on time. So, I ran the rest of the way to the school.

I couldn't concentrate at all during the school day. Normally school dragged on, but today it went by in a flash. The only thoughts going through my mind were what I was going to say when I got home without Faith.

I stood outside of our house for several minutes, trying to mentally prepare myself for the impending doom of being alone. When I walked through the door, Dad looked at me and back at the TV without saying anything. I went straight to the room and nervously sat on the bed, knowing it was only a matter of time before he realized Faith wasn't coming home.

Finally, in what seemed like an eternity, Dad called me out into the living room. "Where's your sister?"

I stood there in terror. My little malnourished body shook so hard I felt like he could hear my knees rattling. I knew I had to say something, but what should I say? Everything I'd rehearsed in my head during school disappeared. Should I lie and say she just ran away? Should I say I knew about the plan? What's going to happen now? Would he take his anger out on me? Is he going to kill me?

The thoughts screamed like ten different people in my head all at once. Each voice created an instantaneous alternative branch plan for how each statement might fully unfold. Every synapse in my brain felt like it was on fire.

My heart was in my throat, and my voice quivered as I finally blurted out as fast as I could, "She ran away with Mom this morning at the Jack in the Box."

I braced myself for his reaction.

He looked at me for a second with a confused look. "What do you mean she went with your mom?"

I couldn't hold the tears back any longer. They streamed down my face like a raging overflowing river. "She left with Mom on the way to school and said she was never coming back."

Dad leaned back in his recliner. I saw him mentally processing what I just said. His face took on a range of emotion from puzzled, to mad, to nervous. He especially seemed nervous because he knew she was free to tell the truth and go to the cops about what he was doing to both of us.

He leaned in and, in the first tender moment I'd had in a year, said, "Thank you for staying, son."

I cried hysterically at this point, confused in the moment of tenderness from him, but devastated I'd just lost my sister without knowing if I'd ever see her again.

———

Patrick had moved back just before Faith left because Gail went into the hospital for a drug overdose and couldn't take care of him anymore. He was only four, so he didn't understand what was going on, just confused that his sister wasn't there.

Dad sat despondent for the next hour and didn't say anything. I could tell he was trying to put the pieces together and make sense of it all. Dad told me to start dinner and said he would be back later. He needed to be by himself for a while.

I filled a pot of water and put it on the stove. I started sobbing uncontrollably. My tears and emotions boiled over like the water in front of me. Dad didn't come back to the house to eat the spaghetti I cooked. Instead, he went to the bar and didn't come back until we'd fallen asleep that night.

Watching Patrick eat at the table that night, I knew I was now the oldest sibling in the house and needed to protect Patrick like Faith tried to protect me. I took on the role of protector for my little brother that day even though I was a scared, emotional, and unprepared ten-year-old boy.

The following week, the school administrator called over the loudspeaker into my classroom, "Please send Walter to the principal's office as soon as possible."

I wasn't sure what this was about, but thought it probably had something to do with Faith or that Mom came back to get me. The kids snickered, thinking I was in trouble, which was normal anytime someone was called the office. But I knew I wasn't.

The guidance counselor was waiting to greet me when I entered the office. She had a disarming smile on her face and asked me to follow her into a conference room next to the principal's office.

I walked in and saw two police officers sitting at the conference table. I stopped in my tracks and suddenly wanted to run. The counselor bumped into me from behind and nudged me forward. The officers stood up to greet me and shake my hand.

I looked at the counselor and asked her if I was in trouble and going to jail. My young brain struggled to process what was happening. She smiled and told me the officers were there to ask me a few questions. I stared at the officers and saw their stern faces became soft and compassionate. One of them reached down with his left hand to turn his squawking walkie-talkie off. Everything was moving in slow motion and the realness of the situation grabbed hold of me.

One officer asked me to sit in a chair and pulled another one up right next to me while the other officer sat across the table. I felt like I was going to throw up. I wanted to go home because I knew they were going to ask questions about Faith.

The officer started talking. "I want you to know you are not in any trouble. We're going to ask you about things happening at your house that were reported to us. I want you to be honest with me. Our only job is to make sure you're safe. We will protect you."

My body trembled and I felt mentally stuck in place. I wanted to cry out that I needed help but just sat there, paralyzed with fear. I nodded my head while they talked so they knew I understood them.

"Your sister and Mom filed a complaint with the police that your dad was abusing the two of you and you weren't safe living with him. Can you talk to us about what's happening?"

I was nervous, which caused me to stutter. I looked down at my shoes and swiveled back and forth in my chair, trying to find the right words before saying in a meek voice, "I don't know anything."

The officer, aware I was scared, touched my hand. "Son, it's OK. Nothing bad is going to happen to you. You are not in any trouble. We know what's going on in your house and just need you to tell us the truth."

I couldn't look up and just kept staring at the ground, contemplating what to say next. My palms felt clammy against the chair and beads of sweat appeared on my forehead.

"Have you ever seen your dad touch your sister in the private area or has he touched you in yours?" The officer asked.

I told him no. Dad didn't touch me in my privates and I never saw him do it to Faith. I wanted to yell out that I believed Faith and Dad was a monster, but was mentally and emotionally shut down because of my fear.

The officer sighed and asked, "Has your dad ever smacked, punched, kicked or hit you with a belt?"

I felt my face go flush and turn as red as the chair I was sitting on. My internal struggle of fear and truth battled inside of me, causing me to tremble all over.

The officer reached down and lightly touched my bruised wrist. "What happened there?"

I flinched from the pain and lied again. "I fell outside playing during recess."

He tried to reassure me of my safety and said he'd ask me one more time, "Has your dad ever hit you or Faith?"

I was crying uncontrollably now but couldn't muster up the courage to speak my truth. Fear was my master, and I couldn't overcome it. "Dad doesn't hit us," barely came out of my mouth. I knew it was an outright lie.

The officers knew I was scared and could see my heart beating out of my chest but were at a loss of what to do next. He turned to the other officer and whispered something in his ear. The other officer, who'd been quiet until this point, tried to ask the same questions in a different way and continued to reiterate I'd be safe if I told them what was happening. He told me that parents shouldn't hit their kids and, if that was happening, I had to let them help me get out.

My dad held ultimate power and fear over me. The belief that he would hurt me if I spoke the truth was so strong, I denied everything. Both of the officers shook their heads in disbelief and turned to the counselor saying there was nothing more they could do. The first officer shook my hand again and told me to let the school counselor or principal know if anything changed and he would come back to help me.

The counselor told me I could sit in her office until I was ready to go back to class.

I sat in her office for a while, unable to move. I couldn't shake the feeling I'd missed my opportunity to run again. Plus, I felt ashamed for lying. I felt a strong sense of distrust because every adult I knew up until this point lied, beat, yelled, or hurt me in some way.

I wanted to believe the officers could help me. But I couldn't even trust my own parents, so how could I trust two total strangers? The grim reality I would probably never get a chance to tell my truth again, and

I'd be with Dad until I turned 18, hit me like a ton of bricks.

I felt more lost than I'd ever been.

CHAPTER 10

RUNNING FROM PROSECUTION

CPS came to do a health and welfare check a week after I'd been questioned at school.

Dad was not happy they were coming to the house. He warned Patrick and I beforehand, "You better both tell them your life is incredible living with me and how well I take care of you. If either of you say anything wrong, I will beat you until you can't stand once they leave."

I knew to say things were fine and coached Patrick, who was only five, to say the same things as me. The CPS visit went as planned. Dad turned on the charm, while Patrick and I just nodded in agreement or answered that everything was fine.

The day after CPS came to our house, Dad walked in and set three duffle bags in the middle of the living room floor next to where Pat and I were playing Army men.

"I can't find another job and I need help watching you two. We're going to move close to our family in

Yuma, Arizona. Plus, I'm not going to have CPS snooping around and trying to take me to jail. We're getting the hell out of here."

———

I didn't know my dad's family very well. I only saw them sporadically in my first ten years of life, but the vague memories I did have of my grandmother trying to protect me and being kind were enough to make me excited.

Our car wasn't running anymore so Dad told us to only pack our clothes and a couple of toys. I asked what was going to happen to all of our stuff. He said our uncle was going to bring everything to us in a moving truck in a few weeks.

The next day, my uncle drove us to downtown San Diego and dropped us off at the Greyhound bus station. I'd never ridden on a Greyhound bus before, but Dad told me it was fun and we could meet new people on the ride. He said the bus's big windows made the ride better because we could see all the scenery for miles. He told me we'd be fine on the bus, and I'd sit next to Patrick so I could help keep him calm.

We entered the bus terminal and sat on the benches, waiting for our bus to depart a couple hours later. Patrick had an extreme case of ADHD because of the drugs Gail did while she was pregnant with him. He started to spiral. The chaos of the bus terminal and all the commotion around us made him incredibly hyper. I reached into one of the duffle bags and gave Patrick a Ritalin pill to calm him down. I knew he wouldn't sit still if I didn't.

Dad joined a group of people near where we were sitting and talked with another man. The man looked like a veteran and wore a green Army jacket like I'd seen Dad wear in the past. The man's long beard touched his shirt. He kept pulling a small bottle of Jack Daniel's whiskey from the jacket breast pocket and offering it to my dad. They seemed like they were long-lost buddies, both of them talking and exchanging stories of serving in the Army.

The volume of their voices grew louder in the terminal as the bottle of whiskey disappeared. I wondered how the ride to Yuma would go if Dad was drunk. I knew he became more volatile when he was wasted.

Dad walked over. "I'm going to run to the liquor store across the street to get something for the road. Keep a close eye on your brother until I come back."

It took a while, but I heard him come back into the terminal, laughing and carrying on with his new friend and a couple of other people who joined them. The terminal loudspeaker boomed that bus number seven was departing to Yuma in fifteen minutes and to bring all luggage to the bus. Dad wasn't paying attention. I tapped him on the arm and told him it was time to leave. He looked back at his new friends to say he'd see them onboard and to save him a seat.

He was a bit wobbly, and the whiskey smell emanated from every pore in his body. But he managed to help me corral the bags over to the bus. He threw them near the bus driver who was loading the bags into the storage compartments. The driver looked up when Dad hit him in the leg with one of the bags.

Dad turned back towards him. "What? Do you have a problem?"

The driver shook his head but didn't say anything back. I was full of dread. I knew the five-hour ride was going to feel like an eternity. Pat was tough to keep calm if he didn't have room to run around and Dad was already acting like a drunk maniac.

I felt slightly relieved as the bus lifted its suspension, released its air brakes, and we started our trip.

A man in the back yelled out to Dad, "Hurry up, Walt. You better come get some before it's gone!"

Dad leaned over. "I'm going to the back of the bus with my friends. You keep Patrick in his seat. Neither of you will like it if I have to come back up here."

The stench of whiskey on his breath and the look in his eye let me know he'd hit us in front of everyone if we interrupted his fun. The familiar black label and dark liquid of the Jack Daniel's whiskey bottle the man held up told me Dad's level of drunkenness was only beginning and the night was going to end in catastrophe.

The bus ride was horrendous. Dad and his friends started getting really loud and rowdy in the back. There were quite a few people cautiously looking over their shoulders at all of them, but they were met with the threat of violence if they didn't turn back around.

The driver stopped the bus twice in the middle of the desert and threatened to kick them off the bus if they didn't settle down. Patrick was restless and hungry, too. I could tell his medicine was wearing off, but the rest of it was under the bus in our bags and I didn't have access to it. I was so mad at myself for not making sure we had extra Ritalin for the trip. I was becoming extraordinarily exhausted from all the commotion and tension.

Patrick ran up and down the aisles, uncontrollably yelling and wanting to get off the bus. Dad walked towards us from the back and jerked Patrick's arm as he came down the aisle towards our seats. Dad bent down towards my face so he was at eye level, and squeezed my cheeks really hard.

"If I have to come back here one more time, I will beat you in front of everyone. Patrick, if you get up again, your ass is mine, boy."

Dad's glaring eyes told me everything I needed to know. This was a final warning to get Patrick back in his seat before he'd hit both of us.

We finally stopped in a small town, El Centro, for fifteen minutes about an hour outside of Yuma. I told Dad that we were hungry and asked for a couple of dollars so I could go into the Chevron gas station and buy something for us to eat.

I told Patrick, "Bro, if you calm down, I'll get you something to eat and let you run around for a few minutes before the bus leaves."

Thankfully, it was the only invitation Patrick needed and he took off down the aisle of the bus. He jumped off the steps to the asphalt of the parking lot. I chased him around the gas pumps until I finally caught him and grabbed his hand, terrified he would get hit by a car if I didn't keep ahold of him.

I grabbed us both a couple of hotdogs and we made our way back outside the store just as the bus driver gave a five-minute departure notification. Patrick ran around on the side of the parking lot until it was time to go. He was still so full of uncontrollable energy.

The next hour was a living hell. My brother threw his crayons and kicked the seats in front of him. Dad was even louder in the back of the bus as he became more inebriated. Patrick kept kicking the seat of the man in front of us and I could tell he was becoming pissed. I tried to hold Patrick's legs down, but it only made it worse. Finally, the man in front of Patrick abruptly turned around to yell at us.

He caught me off guard and I flinched, bringing up my hands to block the man from hitting us. Dad saw me flinch and immediately stood up from his seat and yelled at the man. "Who the fuck told you to talk to my kids! You want to try and intimidate someone? Now I'm going to beat your ass in front of everyone when we get off the bus. If you don't turn around, I'll take you out right now."

The bus driver told them both to sit back down because we were almost to Yuma. I saw the city lights of Yuma twinkling in the night. The dark desert landscape made driving up towards a city even brighter than normal. I was thankful we were almost to our destination so I could get out of this crazy and spiraling environment. I wanted to emotionally explode. I couldn't take much more of the uncontrollable situation and cramped quarters anymore.

We pulled into the Yuma bus station. I felt a sense of relief cascade over me knowing my family was there to pick us up. They could help take care of Patrick and Dad. We didn't realize it, but the driver called ahead to the Yuma bus terminal to complain about my dad who'd grown out of control and belligerent with anyone who dared look his way.

Multiple officers were waiting outside the terminal as we exited the bus and took tactical positions around Dad. The previous week, another officer was killed at the bus station following an altercation with a passenger, so the officers were tense and on extremely high alert.

The officers immediately grabbed Dad as we exited the bus and pulled him over to the side to detain him. I knew it wasn't going to end well because my dad was standing in a defensive position, puffing his chest out and balling his fists up while he talked to them. The officers were visibly agitated and told Dad they would arrest him if he didn't calm down.

I stood there crying and pleading. "Dad, just stop! Please listen to them before they hurt you!"

"Fuck you, pigs. You don't know who you're dealing with." Dad yelled at the officers.

They slammed him against the bus. One officer pressed Dad's face against the bus while the other put him in handcuffs. Patrick and I watched in horror. I didn't want to see Dad get hurt, but deep down it felt good to see him being treated like he treated us.

Just then, Aunt Dianna came around the corner. The officers forced Dad to sit on the curb. She immediately tried to defuse the situation. Dad was wasted, had a wild-eyed look of a crazy man, kept calling the officers pigs, and told them to go fuck themselves. I thought he was going to jail.

Patrick spun out of control, feeding off the negative energy and commotion surrounding us. He took off running. I ran to catch him as Aunt Dianna continued to negotiate with the cops.

"I'm taking them all home. We'll leave immediately if you let him go," she told them.

I didn't know her extremely well, but I was so thankful she was there. Aunt Dianna is Dad's youngest sister and only nine years older than me. At twenty, she was already a very strong woman. She had long blond hair and crystal blue eyes. She also had the mouth of a sailor and a heart of gold, a true force to be reckoned with but balanced with an extremely caring heart. Her husband, Rick, drove with her to pick us up. Rick is only about 5'7" tall, but he is a strong guy due to working in landscaping and as a beer deliveryman. He was a lot of fun to be around and would do anything to protect his family, especially Aunt Dianna.

She reaffirmed to the officers that my dad was her older brother and she could handle it from this point. Even through his inebriated belligerence and disrespect, the officers let him go with her and we left immediately. We hustled to the parking lot and got into her car. She had a blue Toyota Corolla hatchback just big enough for us all to fit in. Patrick, Dad, and I sat in the back while Rick drove and Aunt Dianna sat in the passenger seat.

We drove out of the parking lot and my dad, still steaming from his interaction with the police, turned his anger on Aunt Dianna.

"Who in the fuck do you think you are? You and this fucking family are always trying to control things!"

"Knock it off, Walt. You're not being rational because you're drunk. They were about to take you to jail."

Dad pushed her in the back of the head. "You haven't seen irrational yet." He then slapped the side of her face and knocked her glasses off.

Rick flipped out and jumped the curb next to a giant dirt lot. He pulled the emergency brake and the car slid sideways before coming to a complete stop. A giant plume of dirt flew into the sky, and everyone jumped out of the car.

Rick headed towards Dad on the other side of the car. "I've had enough! You want to hit my wife? Then I have something for you!"

Aunt Dianna jumped between them to stop the fight. As Rick tried to grab Dad, my Uncle John came barreling out of nowhere. Apparently, Aunt Dianna had called him from the payphone at the bus terminal. Uncle John raced into the dirt lot, jumped out of his car, and grabbed Dad. This startled Dad long enough to break him out of his drunken rage.

In the turmoil, Pat's ADHD reached a frenzied state. He ran around the car in circles. I stood frozen and watched as everything unfolded in front of me. My mind was focused clearly on everyone's faces, but the surroundings in my peripheral view were fuzzy. I heard Rick yell and I turned my attention back to Patrick, who was hanging for his life from my aunt's car.

Somehow Patrick had released the emergency brake and the car moved forward. He had a white knuckled grip on the steering wheel but was quickly losing his grasp. His body slid out of the car and his foot was just inches away from the back tire. Rick sprung into action and raced to grab Pat just as he couldn't hold on any longer, snatching his belt as he fell out of the car, mere millimeters away from being maimed or killed.

Uncle John pushed Dad towards his car to get him out of the parking lot. He'd noticed the red and blue lights of the police coming towards us. The same officers who almost arrested Dad just a few minutes ago pulled into the parking lot to investigate the plume of smoke and lights. Uncle John sped away with Dad just as the officers arrived, preventing him from being taken to jail.

Aunt Dianna noticed me frozen, unable to move or even react to the situation. She put her arm around me and let me know everything was going to be OK. Dad's brothers and sisters would take care of him now. I was still in shock and so exhausted from the drunken bus ride, Dad's rage, and Patrick wildly out of control. I sat in complete silence the entire car ride to Uncle John's house where my grandma and all the aunts and uncles had an emergency family meeting to try to set my dad straight.

———

Ultimately, we settled in a town called Winterhaven, just on the California border and across the Colorado River from Yuma. Its population of 190 people were primarily Native American since it was built near a reservation. We were some of the only white people who lived there. There was one road through town and no stoplights. It had one small family-owned grocery store and a corner gas station where my dad would inevitably get his beer.

Our house was small, old, and extremely worn. It had two bedrooms and one bathroom with rusted pipes that spewed brown water most of the time. It also had an air conditioner that struggled to keep up with the 110+ degree temperatures, making the inside constantly feel like an oven.

This was our new home, but the house needed to be condemned. The first time we entered the house was shocking. We pushed our way through the six-foot chain-link fence and into the dirt yard. There was an overgrown sissoo tree towering over the entire structure.

It was night, but I could see the pink color of the house through the yellow hue of the porch light. Dad opened the front door and turned on the lights. The entire house looked like it was moving and alive with different sized roaches on every wall, floor, and ceiling, each of them scrambling to find some place to hide from the light. I looked in horror at the number of bugs in the house. We almost always lived someplace with roaches, but this was so much worse than anything I imagined.

Pat screamed and jumped around the entrance, wildly tossing his hair as a roach fell from the ceiling onto his head. I shuddered and felt like throwing up. I wondered how we were going to live here with this many bugs. We walked through the house, towards the kitchen, and turned on the light. It had even more bugs than the living room. Thousands of roaches ran back into the cabinets and sink drains.

Dad told us to go back to the front yard. He would drop bug bombs in every room. As we stood outside, I heard the bombs pop when he opened them. After about a minute, he rushed out of the house.

A cloud of smoke billowed behind him as he closed the front door. Dad saw the look of terror and disgust on our faces and knew we were extremely apprehensive about moving into the house. He told us the bombs would kill the roaches. I hoped he was right.

———

Over the next few weeks, we slowly got more furniture from family, friends, or Goodwill for our house and stored it in my uncle's garage until we got enough to move into our new place. I just wanted to be settled for once, I was so tired from moving multiple times.

I felt extreme anticipation when we pulled back up in front of the pink house, wondering what we'd see and hoping the bugs were killed. We walked in the house. The chemical smell of the bug bombs still permeated the of air. There were dead bugs everywhere and only a few live ones left. This made me feel better. We spent the next couple of days sweeping the floors and cleaning the entire house to prepare for our furniture.

———

A few weeks later, we started a new school again. Since the population was smaller, we shared a campus with kindergarten through eighth grade. Luckily, I was in sixth grade and they kept middle schoolers separate from the elementary students.

I was really thankful that I'd made friends with another eleven year old, Jeff, before school had started. He lived across the street. I didn't know anyone else, but he knew a lot of the kids at school and introduced me to all of his friends in the neighborhood, too.

Jeff quickly became my best friend. We had free reign over the small town because neither of our parents really cared what we did as long as we stayed outside. We spent our days riding bikes and playing video games, but our favorite thing to do was watch WWF. Jeff, I, and all of the neighborhood boys were enthralled by the giant figures we'd see throwing each other around the ring on TV. Hulk Hogan and Hulkamania were at their peak but there were so many other larger-than-life personalities. Like my favorite, the Ultimate Warrior.

The two of us, and the neighborhood kids, would wrestle every extra second we had. We'd throw each other into trees, suplex each other onto beds, and fake punch each other, replicating everything we'd see our heroes do. Our bodies would fake convulse with every hit and we'd all exaggerate the movements just like we'd seen on TV. Sometimes we'd get hurt, but most of the time it was a blast.

———

I was responsible for all of the household chores. Most days were spent cooking, cleaning, and taking care of Pat when I wasn't in school. Dad's rule was that all chores needed to be completely done before I would be allowed to go outside. I also had to be back home in time to cook dinner. At least, when we had food.

Pat was a handful and his ADHD made it extremely difficult to keep him under control. Often, he'd go into a spiral of energy, unable to control himself. His body would shake because he couldn't sit still. Even though Patrick was difficult to take care of, he was my brother and it was my responsibility to make sure he was bathed, fed, and, most importantly, protected from Dad.

One day, I woke up to a commotion in the kitchen. I saw the light turned on just outside our bedroom door. I could tell Pat was up really early again, so I walked out into the kitchen to check on him. I was struggling to wake up. It was 4:30 in the morning and I felt especially sleepy. He always woke up way earlier than anyone else and would get into anything sugary he could get his hands on.

Today was no exception. I turned the corner and saw him sitting on the table. He was straddling the tin container of Nestlé Nesquik chocolate milk powder between his legs and eating it with a spoon. He looked up and I saw his entire mouth caked with the powder stuck on it.

Instantly, I knew it was going to be another long morning. I quickly gave him his ADHD medicine so he wouldn't wake Dad up and get us both in trouble, afraid of the beating we'd get if he came around the corner and saw what was happening.

As I started waking up, I noticed the distinct chemical smell of Raid fill my nostrils and become more prominent by the second. I looked at Pat and asked him if he was spraying the Raid. He would do that from time to time if he saw roaches. His eyes got big, and he started laughing hysterically. My hair felt itchy and my scalp felt like it was on fire. I started to scratch my head and smelled my hands. The stench overpowered me instantly.

I grabbed Pat by the shirt and asked if he sprayed Raid into my hair, which was now becoming incredibly uncomfortable. I walked back into the room and saw the can of bug spray by my pillow, solidifying my assumption. Patrick laughed as I ran to the shower to wash it off. It took me five washes in a row until the smell finally came out of my hair. I came out of the bathroom and Pat asked if I was going to tell Dad. I told him no but also that he was a pain in the ass. Freaking brothers sometimes!

———

Pat and I stayed away from Dad and played outside every day. I brought Pat with me wherever I went. I knew Dad would beat him if he was in the house by himself.

At this point, Dad was a full-blown alcoholic and spent most of his time either in the recliner or on his bed, often passed out from too many beers or prescription drugs. He'd yell and carry on when he was inebriated, often throwing things and hitting us with his belt, fists, sometimes even extension cords.

This went on for months until one day I realized Dad hadn't come out of his room for a few days. We never really knew what he was doing in his room but knew for sure there was no way we were going to knock on the door. But something didn't feel right, so I decided to go in.

It felt hot in the room. Dad was asleep. He felt like he was on fire. His hair was matted on his head. I pushed his arm and yelled, but he wouldn't move. He only mumbled incoherently. On one hand, I felt relieved that he wasn't hitting us. But, on the other, I was worried about what was wrong with him.

We didn't have any food in the house except some instant potatoes and a can of peas. I knew that was going to run out by the following day. I rushed to the payphone at the corner store to ask Aunt Dianna for help.

I loved Aunt Dianna. She was so kind to us. She always stopped by our place, driving about an hour from her house to check and make sure Patrick and I were OK. She knew the things my dad was capable of, and even tried to get Dad to let us live with her. But he got furious when she asked. She was only twenty-one at the time. I know, if she had had the means, she would have taken Dad to court for custody.

Aunt Dianna was quick to come over when I called. She drove the hour from her house to see what was going on. When she arrived, she took Dad's temperature. It was 105 degrees. She tried to get him to sit up, but he was hallucinating and severely dehydrated.

She told Patrick and me to pack some clothes. "We need to take your dad to the emergency room because he isn't going to make it if we don't. You guys are coming home with me."

Dad was admitted to the hospital upon arrival. Doctors descended on him from multiple areas and took him to the ICU as soon as they saw him. He spent the next week in the hospital with an intestinal infection. Meanwhile, we stayed at Aunt Dianna's.

We found out later that Dad had actually died in the ICU. But the doctors resuscitated him, bringing him back to life and pumping massive amounts of antibiotics into his system.

———

I had so much peace and joy at Aunt Dianna's that I didn't want to ever leave. She took care of Patrick so I could relax and be a normal kid for the first time in my life. She helped us with our homework, hugged and loved on us, and made sure we had a warm meal.

After eleven years of tyrannical abuse, this was the first taste of normal family life I ever experienced. I was hungry for more. Even Patrick was calmer and doing well in school. The routine and love given to us helped immensely. But it was short lived.

When Dad came to pick us up, he seemed even angrier at the world than he normally did. I watched through the trailer window as he yelled at Aunt Dianna for no apparent reason.

He threw open the trailer door. "Get your shit and get in the car now."

Aunt Dianna tried to talk him into letting us stay. I prayed she could talk him into letting us stay with her. But he acted like the request was a giant conspiracy to take us away from him. I didn't want to go and wished that he just left Patrick and I there.

I was pissed that he treated her so poorly after the love she'd given us. I didn't even realize I was doing it initially, but I glared at him when he got back into the car, unable to control my anger. He looked over at me and said that he'd beat any problems out of me. He then backhanded me in the face like he'd done a thousand times before. I melted back into the passenger seat in a ball of tears and didn't look at him again the rest of the ride back home.

———

A few months later, Dad's California disability entitlement ran out. So, he told us we were leaving again, this time closer to Yuma. I was happy we were moving this time. I hated the rusty water, roaches, and tiny town we lived in. Outside of my friends, there was nothing to do. I was also excited to live closer to Grandma Flo and Aunt Dianna.

———

Dad got a job at the Yuma Proving Grounds, an Army base just outside of Yuma and one of the best places to work. He leveraged his disabled veteran status to get a role in the tank gunner shop shooting tank rounds like he did when he was active duty in the Army. He was happy and I was ecstatic he got a good job. This meant we'd have money for food, a nicer place to live, and I'd see him a lot less because he'd be at work.

The only downside to moving was I had to switch schools again. But after being in nine schools in seven years, I was used to it. Since it was seven-to-eighth grade, everyone was new to the school and needed to make friends, so the move didn't bother me nearly as much as before.

With Dad working, I turned into the full-time maid, cook, babysitter, and mom of the house. I was required to cook, clean, do laundry, and take care of Pat every day until he got home from work or returned from the bar. Even though Dad made way more money in this job, we never benefited from it. Sometimes we'd have food, but Dad still chose to drink away the money. We ended up broke a few days before payday, which meant we'd have nothing to eat for a few days. I knew something had to change.

I wanted to start earning my own money. Dad didn't buy us the things we needed, so I told him I wanted a paper route to earn extra money. I figured since most of the route was in the apartment complex and adjacent neighborhoods, I could ride my bike around to deliver the newspaper. On top of taking care of the house, I grew my paper route from 90 to 211 customers, going door-to-door to ask if they'd sign up.

I'd get up at 4 in the morning on the weekend. During the week, I'd hustle home after school to wrap stacks of papers dropped on my doorstep with rubber bands. I fit them neatly into a bag and wrapped it around my grey BMX bicycle handlebars. Since I had the paper route money, I'd buy Pat and I food to cook for dinners. We'd finally have something to eat other than just the free lunch we got at school. I was good at only keeping enough food in the house for just the two of us, even hiding some in my room. Dad would eat it all when he was drunk.

Eventually, Dad realized I was buying food and making more money than he thought.

"Boy, you're twelve now. You should start paying your fair share in this house. You shouldn't have money to spend on whatever you want. I need more money for my bar tab and you're going to supplement it with the paper route money."

I was so angry! I knew there was nothing I could say without being hit. At the risk of getting beat, I started hiding half the tip money under my dresser where I hoped he couldn't find it.

The following summer, Dad was passed over for promotion at YPG and sued the government, saying he wasn't hired because of nepotism. When I saw the eviction notice on the table, Dad said we were moving across to the other side of Yuma. He couldn't afford the rent anymore.

He told Patrick that he was moving back in with his mom, Gail. "I can't handle your hyperactivity anymore. It's her turn to take care of you."

I couldn't believe he could just throw his children away. He was doing the same thing to Patrick that he did to Faith and me. Even though Patrick was difficult, he was my brother and I loved him.

I had a really difficult time when he left. This was the second time a sibling was ripped out of my life due the selfishness of our parents.

I knew being alone with Dad was going to come with its own challenges.

CHAPTER 11
JUSTICE

We moved into the Country Club apartments—a one bedroom, one bathroom, 800 square foot rundown apartment complex. Since it was out of the Crane school district, I had to switch schools again for eighth grade. I'd now be going to Gila Vista Junior High and starting all over, once again, in a new school. Dad was gone a lot which I was thankful for because if he wasn't home then he wasn't hitting me, and if he came home drunk, I would act like I was asleep, which prevented drunken beatings most of the time.

After a few months in our new place, Dad introduced me to his new girlfriend, Cindy. He'd met her at his favorite bar, The Showcase Lounge, and they quickly jumped headfirst into a serious relationship. She was nice to me, and Dad was a lot less angry when she was around, so I liked when she came over. Cindy and Dad's relationship seemed good when they were sober but turned tumultuous whenever they got drunk. I hated when she'd barge out of the house to go home after pissing my dad off because the beatings I took following their arguments were even worse than normal. He'd be in a rage and unable to control his emotions, oftentimes hitting me with his belt or anything else within reach until I cowered on the floor. During this time, it didn't matter what was happening if he was triggered, the response was always to hit me. I was getting desperate and didn't know how much longer I could take the chaos. I had to dig deep into my spirit to keep going.

He also became like a drill sergeant and seemed to be looking for anything I did wrong so he could abuse me. Every night when I was done cooking and cleaning up after dinner, Dad would come into the kitchen to inspect the dishes. He'd run his finger around the top, sides, and underneath the plates and pots searching for specks of food or grease. I prayed he wouldn't find anything as I stood there wanting to shrivel up and disappear.

On one occasion, I could tell he was already in a bad mood and looking extra hard to find something wrong. He picked up a cast iron skillet and held it up to the light. I stood there for what seemed like an eternity, waiting for permission to go to my room as his eyes covered every inch of the skillet. He turned it to the left and I saw a glimmer of light hit a small patch of grease. I wished I'd checked it one more time before calling him in to inspect.

He swooshed his finger around the bottom of the pan and held it out so I could see.

"What the hell did I tell you about making sure these were clean?" he said to me in a low evil grumble, his crazed eyes preparing me for the inevitable.

I felt defeated, like I couldn't do anything right, and started to tear up while mentally preparing for my beating. He took his finger and wiped the grease on my face, pressing it against my cheek until I fell backwards against the refrigerator. The next moment shocked me.

He swung the heavy cast iron skillet towards my head. It came at me in what felt like slow motion. I couldn't move fast enough to get out of the way. The pain shot through my entire body as the skillet hit my right temple, shaking me to my core and immediately knocking me down to one knee. My eyes felt like they spun inside their sockets. I was instantly nauseous.

He grabbed my face just under my chin and tilted my head back. His eyes showed no remorse.

Peering down at me, he told me, "You're going to make me kill you if you don't get your shit together," before letting me go and walking out of the room.

I went to the bedroom and laid on the bed in the dark, wondering how much longer I could endure this. My head hurt, my heart hurt, my body hurt and, most of all, my soul hurt. I just didn't want to be alive anymore. I found resilience during these times. I knew once I had control of my own life everything would be different and if I just hung on a little longer, I could make it out of the darkness.

In these dark days, I transported myself into my adult life and imagined what it would be like. I envisioned having a family and being a successful business owner one day. I imagined happy faces and a lot of laughter. I imagined a life where I was big enough to protect myself and others. These images and videos I played in my mind were some of the first instances of manifesting a life I wanted. They kept me alive and looking towards the future during some really dark days.

A few months later, Dad came home on a Wednesday night and told me he was going out of town on Thursday for the weekend. He told me that he and Cindy were going to California. He elaborated that they would spend some time at the beach, go to a baseball game, and finish the trip by going to Disneyland for the day. I didn't know where he got the money from, but I didn't care in the moment.

"Disneyland? Are you kidding me?" I said out loud before continuing on, "I won't miss any important tests at school and, since we'll be back by Monday for basketball practice, the timing is perfect!"

Dad looked at the TV for a minute and turned to me. "What makes you think you're going?"

I was stunned and didn't know what to say. The pit in my stomach grew as I realized he wasn't going to take me.

I softly told him, "I assumed you were going to take me, too," holding just an ounce of hope I might get to still go.

Without hesitation, he replied, "You're an idiot for thinking I would take you. I love *her*, so why would I take *you*?"

He turned back and started watching TV again. I leaned into my chair and held back tears of pain and the words of anger I felt. I was devastated! I wondered why he hated me so much and why he made it a point to make me feel this way all the time. I started to hate him just as much as he hated me.

———

Cindy arrived at the house and they got ready to hit the road. Both of them were hugging and kissing each other as Dad packed his suitcase. Their excitement for the trip and outwardly way they rejoiced in front of me made me feel like they were rubbing it in. Dad stopped on the way out the door and told Cindy he'd be downstairs in a minute.

He looked over to me. "If you call anyone in the family while I'm gone, I'll fucking kill you when I get back. Got it?!"

The smug look on his face made me want to push him off the balcony. I was so angry. Instead, I looked back at him with the saddest thirteen-year-old eyes in history and nodded my head in agreement. I thought about Mom, who I hadn't seen in over four years, and my siblings. I wondered if they felt as destitute as I did. It was one of the worst moments of my life. My heart was weary and broken as I cried myself to sleep that night. I'd never felt so alone.

The next day after school, I sat by myself in the apartment with my emotions on a rollercoaster, ebbing and flowing from pissed, sad, angry, hurt, and dejected, to feeling like I wasn't good enough to be loved. I sat on the edge of the bed, crying again for most of the night and wondering why my entire life had been so terrible.

I woke up on Saturday morning and decided I was going to kill myself. I wrote a suicide note and included drawings of a kid shooting himself. I told Dad in the letter that he was responsible for my terrible life and because he and Mom didn't love me, I was going to make things easy for them. I wanted both of them, but especially Dad, to know they were responsible for my death. I placed the note on Dad's pillowcase so he'd find it when he returned from California.

I walked into the kitchen and stared at the butcher block of knives, trying to muster up the courage to grab one. A flood of memories ran through my mind like a movie. I could vividly hear all my abusers clearly:

"I'm going to kill you."

"You're so scared all the time."

"You're never going to be anything."

"You're a piece of shit."

"I can't believe I'm stuck with you fucking kids."

"I don't know where you got your big nose and gap teeth from. It sure wasn't from me because I'm not ugly like you."

"I love *her*, so why would I take *you*?"

My blood boiled. I was in a rage as I relived the years of torture I'd endured...

Years thrown in a basement...

Being pinned down with splinters put under my fingernails...

Blistered lips from hot water...

Slapped.

Punched.

Kicked.

Belittled.

Abandoned.

And neglected.

I screamed incoherently as I stood in the kitchen and yelled out, "I wish you all would go to hell for what you did to me! You'll see what it's like when I'm dead and really not here anymore!"

I grabbed the largest knife from the butcher block as my pain and anger became frenzied enough to give me the courage to take my life. I stomped into the bathroom with purpose and intention and put my left arm palm up over the bathroom sink. I felt my heart pumped faster than it ever had, my face flush and red, the veins in my wrists bulging and pulsating as my mind raced into overdrive.

My mind screamed out, *Do it! End it all now and you won't be in pain anymore.*

I moved my right hand with the knife towards my left wrist and pressed the tip into my flesh, breaking the skin. The pain felt good in the moment. I wondered if my parents would be devastated when they found out I was dead and hoped this would hurt them like they hurt me.

The next moments can only be described as intensely spiritual. I know now that God was with me in the bathroom that day. I was determined to commit suicide and tried to press the knife further into my skin, but I heard someone whisper into my ear to stop. There was nobody in the apartment so it shocked me, especially because now I felt paralyzed and couldn't move. I felt a strong hand wrap around mine and pull the knife away from my wrist. Time stood still for what seemed like an eternity. A warm feeling flooded my body. It felt like the sun on the first warm day of spring, and a sense of peace came over me.

The peace I felt started to heal my brokenness that day. I couldn't explain it then, but now, as an adult I know, the feeling was God's grace saving my life and blessing me in my darkest hour. I felt like I floated back to the living room. Something inexplicably changed deep inside my soul that day. Somehow, I knew I was going to be OK no matter what happened to me. I closed my eyes and was given a vision of heavy armor being placed over my entire body, protecting me and willing me to continue to stay alive regardless of the hell still coming.

Inside the house was a prison, but outside I could do what I wanted. I lashed out at people, stole whatever I wanted, and ditched school. I fulfilled the stereotype of a kid who comes from a broken home. I knew I wanted more from life; I just didn't know how I was going to get it. Over the next decade, it was an internal battle of will at the center point of my decisions.

———

Cindy and Dad became more serious. As they did, the Mr. Hyde portion of my dad's persona showed itself more often. Their fighting happened multiple times a week, becoming extremely physically and emotionally abusive. Dad slapped, punched or kicked her and she'd get right back up and take swings at him, connecting with more than her fair share. At fourteen, I knew trying to intervene was futile and to get out of the way while they took their drunken rages out on each other. The yelling and stomping would be so loud that the neighbor in the apartment below would hit the ceiling with her broom and from time to time, call the cops. The abuse continued to escalate between Dad and I, too. I was getting bigger, so he'd stand in front of me, measuring me up and taking full swings at me like I was a man.

I took every opportunity to be outside and away from my dad, even if it was sitting in the courtyard of the apartments in the 110-degree Arizona heat. I met a friend named Troy whose family became an extension of mine. I felt safe at Troy's house. I was a nuisance when Cindy was around, so my dad was more than happy to let me go over to Troy's almost anytime I wanted. I practically lived at their house and felt at home when I was there.

Troy's mom, Robin, treated me like one of her own sons, even joking around about adopting me, especially after learning what kind of abuse I endured. Staying at their house gave me a sense of normalcy and peace. It was so much fun hanging out over there. We played hours of basketball and video games while eating all their chips and salsa. During sleepovers, we'd be so loud that Robin would come down in the middle of the night and tell us in her parental voice to "keep it down." It was my safe haven and helped save my life and gave me my first example of what a normal family looked like.

Ditching school and stealing from stores became the norm for me as I lashed out in anger at the world. It didn't matter who I stole from or what I stole, I just enjoyed the rush. My favorite thing to steal was boxes of candy bars from the store. I could sell them the next day at school for $1 each, which was great because I needed the money for food. I was getting exceptionally brazen, just taking anything I wanted and not really caring about the consequences.

My friend, Brian, and I walked around Yuma, ditching another day of school as the end of our eighth-grade year came to a close. It was hot in Yuma and the extreme 110+ degree May temps of the desert made our trek around town almost unbearable. We walked through an apartment complex, its cleanly manicured grass and sparkling blue pool inviting us in to take a cool dip. We didn't have anything better to do, so jumped in.

We opened the gate of the pool and took off our sneakers. The pair of red and white British Knights shoes felt like they were melting on my feet. I took off my shirt and made a mad dash for the pool, jumping headfirst into the deep end. A loud "ah!" left my lips as I came up, the refreshing coolness of the water instantly rinsing away the sticky sweat from the day.

We swam for about fifteen minutes before the manager of the complex came out and asked which apartment we lived in.

He stared at us with his hands on his hips and said, "I know you boys don't live here and if you don't get out of here, I'm going to call the cops for truancy."

That was all I needed to hear. We jumped out of the pool and put our shirts and shoes back on so quickly that water soaked our socks. We ran out of the complex, taking shortcuts through the buildings so the manager couldn't see us anymore. I heard him yell as we turned the corner that we'd be in trouble if he found us in the apartments again.

We neared the end of the complex and stopped running because something else caught our eye. A first-floor apartment on the corner had two pristine road bikes unlocked and sitting out on the front patio just asking for us to steal them. It was hot and I didn't feel like walking all the way back across town, so we agreed to take them. A shot of adrenaline ran through my body as we stood there. I knew it was wrong to steal them, but I really didn't care.

The patio door was closed, but the blinds were open. Even though we couldn't see anyone inside, we were almost certain someone was home. Brian moved first, opening the gate and pushing a bike into my hand before grabbing the second one. We rode the bikes with the precision and speed of a Tour de France rider. I could tell the bikes were expensive because the pedals and gears worked flawlessly together in unison. The wheels turned like they had a motor attached to them, making it easy for the two of us to ride around Yuma for the day.

We rode across town and back towards our apartments to make sure we were home by the time the bus normally dropped us off. I told Brian we should throw the bikes in the orange groves so someone could find them later. We rode the bikes three rows deep into the groves and leaned them against one of the trees. I wanted to make sure they were hidden but still close enough to the sidewalk that someone could see them. Later that night, I started to feel bad for taking the bikes and thought that if I called the police and told them I found them, they would return them to the owner.

I called the police the next morning and told them my friend and I came across two mountain bikes in the orange groves close to my house and they should come get them. The police asked for my name, address, and for us to meet them at the location of the bikes. We met the officers at the orange groves and told them our story about how we found the bikes while taking a shortcut to another neighborhood.

The officers immediately sensed something was off about our story and split us up to ask more questions. It didn't take long to uncover a bull crap story from two kids who were terrible at lying. The officers said our story didn't add up and if we weren't honest with them, they'd charge us for grand theft since the bikes were $1,000 each. Brian and I immediately told the entire story of how we ditched and stole the bikes to joy ride on.

The police officers arrested us, drove us to our houses in separate cop cars, and told our parents what happened. I panicked because I knew Dad's reaction was going to be quick and decisive. I tried to plead with the officer to let me go as he drove me home and told him my dad would beat me if he found out. He told me I probably needed the belt since I was so quick to steal something. He had no way of knowing just how bad it was.

The officers gave us a ticket and eight hours of community service for stealing but didn't charge us with grand theft. I felt like I got off easy by them, but I wasn't so lucky with Dad. Dad thanked the officers for bringing me home and shook their hands. He made sure to keep his composure and was a master at turning his charm on in front of other people. As the officers walked out the door, he gave me one of those bone chilling looks he was so good at. I knew a severe beating was coming.

Dad closed the door and watched while they walked down the stairs. He then stripped off his belt. The familiar sound of the buckle clanging together and the sliding sound of his belt being pulled through the loops on his jeans sent me back into a childlike state. I told him I was sorry and it wouldn't happen again while I slowly backed up towards the bedroom to get away. He snapped the belt forward with a flick of his wrist. It hit me like a whip, square on the nose with the buckle. I grabbed my face. My nose immediately started to bleed and swell up.

"You're damn right you're sorry. You're going to pay for embarrassing me like that. You are the reason Cindy left me and I hate you for it."

I wanted to lash out but couldn't find the voice to do it. I knew Cindy left him because he was hitting her, and I was pissed he tried to blame it on me. I could smell the alcohol on his breath while he swung the belt towards any part of my body he could make contact with. He had no regard for where he hit me or where he swung the belt. He beat me into submission, also breaking a lamp and glass of water sitting on the living room table. I knew he was pissed about me stealing the bikes, but also knew he was far angrier about Cindy leaving him. The reality was his abuse and anger towards life was ruining every relationship he had; Cindy, our family, and me.

———

Even through all of my abuse, Aunt Dianna was never too far away. Although she couldn't figure out a way to permanently take me from Dad, she always showed up randomly to get me from the apartment. She was the only person I had who would listen, the only person in my corner, and the only person who would come to get me when the beatings and yelling became unbearable. Aunt Dianna was always trying to help and became a normal fixture in and around my house after Dad and I moved into the Holiday apartments when I was fifteen. She was only twenty-four and just starting her life, but she couldn't stand the thought of me getting beat like I was.

After one particularly savage beating, I rode my bike as fast as I could to the nearest payphone, a Circle K about a mile from my apartment. I propelled myself forward with hurt and anger. My eyes filled with tears, the extreme Arizona heat dried my mouth, and the hot wind felt like a blow dryer on my face. I was in the same place I'd been so many times before, calling for help after being hit again.

I picked up the receiver with trembling hands and put it to my ear. My voice shook when Aunt Dianna picked up the phone. I told her it happened again, but this time Dad beat me really bad. I explained that he kept punching me in the face and kicking me in the ribs after coming home drunk. I tried to yell back and stand up to him but doing so ended up being a mistake because he wouldn't stop hitting me until he was exhausted. Aunt Dianna said she would be right over to help and for me to go wait on the stairs in front of the apartment.

Dad was awake when she got to the house, so she told him she was taking her son, Brent, to the circus and wanted me to go with them.

"I don't care what you do with his dumbass. Get him out of my face."

A sense of relief came over me when she looked at me and winked after he said I could go. She told Dad she was keeping me for the night and would bring me back the next day.

I felt Aunt Dianna staring at me as we drove; the tenderness in her eyes made me feel safe but was something I was uncomfortable with because I wasn't used to it. My face was already bruising and very swollen from the punches I took but, even worse, my heart was broken. I was desperate for love because I had a father and mother who couldn't show it to me.

"Why is this my life and why can't I just have a normal childhood?" I asked Aunt Dianna. I sat there wondering where my mom was because I hadn't seen her in almost six years. I wondered if she even cared if she had a son or how bad my life was. I took steps forward every day. I knew I only had a couple more years at most with Dad. Then I'd be free to do what I wanted as an adult. I just had to hold out a little longer. I could still feel God's armor protecting me, but it was worn, tattered, and showed signs of fatigue. I stared out the passenger window deep in thought and focused on the expansiveness of the desert. I knew there was a big world beyond what I could see, and I would make up for my lost childhood by exploring it when I was grown.

———

Aunt Dianna, Brent, and I drove past the lettuce fields to meet up with two of my aunts who were visiting a friend's farm. When we arrived, I could see my aunts looking towards me, then back at Aunt Dianna in disbelief at the swelling in my face. Aunt Dianna told them how Dad really beat me badly this time and how she thought he was going to kill me if they didn't do something.

One of my aunts walked over to give me a hug. I didn't know how to show affection and shied away from their physical touch. The way I hugged was by putting one hand on their back from the side and patting them. I just didn't have it in me to wrap my arms around anyone lovingly. I wanted to be able to hug someone normally but didn't know how and it made me uncomfortable. I wished someone would do something. I knew I couldn't take this very much longer. I was holding on and focusing on moving out on my own one day, but it was getting tougher by the day.

Aunt Dianna sat me down that night and said that she couldn't take me getting abused anymore and we needed to do something about it. Dad was becoming increasingly violent with me, and she knew it. She told me she'd been in touch with social services and we had to devise a plan to get me out of Dad's house before he killed me. Aunt Dianna called CPS and spoke with a caseworker who told her the state couldn't remove me from the home unless I was hit after a report was submitted. We both knew the caseworker's answer meant I was going to need to get abused again before I could be removed from Dad's home.

Aunt Dianna started to cry. "I promise, we're going to get you out of there. I'm so sorry, but they won't let me take you unless your dad hits you again. The next time he hits you, I want you to run away as fast as you can. Go to a friend's house and call me. I'll come right over to get you with the cops, and all of this will be over."

I couldn't believe I had to get hit again before the state would remove me from the house. To make matters worse, CPS was going to send a caseworker out to do a welfare check in the next week. I felt like I was back in fourth grade again, terrified my dad would be allowed to retain custody of me. Afraid because he successfully bullied people to get his way so many times before. I felt like he would kill me if CPS did a health and welfare check and I had to stay.

But for the first time in forever, I also felt a sense of hope! It was like seeing the smallest light in the pit of darkness and despair. I wanted to start a new life and I was prepared to get hit one more time to get the hell out of there. I cried myself to sleep that night, my emotions were all over the spectrum. I thought about how this was almost over. After a lifetime of abuse, I could feel freedom from my purgatory inching ever so close. As I laid there, I mentally prepared myself for the inevitable and how I would react once Dad abused me again.

———

Two days later, Dad walked towards me in a military-style march, stomping his feet and yelling at the top of his lungs. "What in the fuck did I tell you, you ignorant no-good piece of shit? I said to not leave the steps, didn't I?"

Just moments ago, he was passed out drunk and high from his prescription medicine, drooling in his recliner in our living room. Five of my friends and I sat on the steps just outside the door to my apartment, laughing and joking with each other without a care in the world.

One of the cute girls I liked grabbed the hat I had on my head and ran into the grass downstairs, giggling, and said, "Come get me."

I thought that this would be my chance to give her a hug. I felt the smile on my face and a rush of emotions came over me as the joy only flirtation can bring filled me.

I quickly jumped up. "You can't outrun me. I'm going to catch you!"

She turned back. "You better hurry!" She sprinted towards the other side of the apartments.

I hurdled down the last four steps and chased her down the street, laughing the entire way. Her blond hair and tanned legs kept my attention as I ran towards her. I finally caught up to her just down the street. She turned towards me and grinned; her smile was like a ray of sunshine straight into my heart. My heart skipped a beat as she gave me a hug. I wanted to kiss her, but our friends ran up right before I had the chance. We held hands as we walked back to my apartment.

Initially, I didn't see Dad walking down the street towards me, but I heard him yelling. My friends and I walked towards him, and I was really embarrassed at his actions. When I got close enough to see his face, I knew he was in an unstoppable emotional rage. My friends looked at me with extreme uncertainty and I shot them a reassuring look, letting them know it would be OK. I was trying to play it cool, but I knew mentally that nothing was actually going to be OK. The next set of events shocked even me because he never hit me in front of anyone before.

I met my dad in the middle of the street right next to the Holiday Apartments office building. "I was just running to get my hat and we were playing around."

He looked at me. "Bullshit. I fucking told you to stay the fuck on the steps. I don't care why you're over here."

I felt like I could crawl under a rock. He was yelling and cussing at me in front of my friends. I was mortified he didn't even care that people were on their evening walks and watching us. I noticed his fists were clenched as he continued his verbal barrage and moved closer to me. He stepped behind me and moved to my right side so he could use his dominant left hand to punch me.

I felt the knuckles of his left hand hit me on the side of my cheek. I stumbled, almost losing my balance and hat in the process. The gasps from my friends were deafening. One of them screamed out "Hey!" I looked at them, startled and dazed, before turning back to Dad in an attempt to re-explain myself. He punched me on the side of my head again, this time knocking my hat to the ground.

The girl I liked screamed out, "Walt, just run!" She was in tears at the abuse she was witnessing.

I bent down on one knee to pick up the hat. I felt the heat radiating off the asphalt from the Arizona sun as I contemplated my next move. I looked back up at Dad and fifteen and a half years of pain, abuse, fear, anger, hurt, and shame surged through my body.

My mind screamed out the conversation with Aunt Dianna two days ago when she said, *The next time he hits you, I want you to run away as fast as you can to anybody's house and call me. I'll come right over to get you with the cops, and all of this will be over.*

Years of emotion coursed through my veins, surging through my body as my pupils widened, my neck pulsated, and my nerve endings made everything tingle. *This is my chance to get away from him and save myself. This is my chance for a new beginning.*

I made a decision as I looked back towards the ground—and ran! My first steps were quick as a cheetah being chased by a lion. I leapt from a knee to a dead sprint all in one motion and ran as fast as my body would carry me.

I heard Dad yelling, "You better get your ass back here, boy! 1! 2! 3!" I didn't turn around.

My friends and I ran a few blocks away and all huddled behind a cinder block fence. We were panting with our hands on our knees and tried to catch our breath.

The girl I liked asked, "What are you going to do?"

"I need to use one of your phones and call my aunt to come get me."

One of my buddies told me we can probably get back to his apartment without my dad finding us. Dad didn't know where he lived, and his place was the closest. The problem we had was the building was only two over from mine.

I could hear my dad frantically yelling as we got closer to the apartments. "Junior, you better get back over here. When I find you, your ass is grass, boy." It was a distant yell but clear as day to me, and, because he was trying to find us, I knew we had to be sneaky getting back to my friend's house.

All six of us slowly crept around the buildings, hiding behind cars in parking spaces, and making sure to look around corners so we were 100% sure we didn't run into my dad. We must have looked like the sneakiest, most silent kids as we made our way to his place, none of us saying a word. We ran through his door and locked it. We were all scared and felt like my dad could bust through the door at any moment.

I picked up the phone and dialed Aunt Dianna. "He hit me again and is looking for me right now. I'm scared he might find us."

"I'm on my way. Stay put inside the apartment until the cops arrive and tell you it's safe to come out."

Fifteen minutes later, we heard a banging at the door.

One of the officers said, "This is the Yuma Police Department. We're looking for Walter McKinley, Jr. Is he in there? It's safe and you can come out now. We're here to protect you." One of the police officers was 6'5" and a mountain of a man. He had a commanding presence with tattoos on his arms and a military style haircut. My intuition told me the officer wouldn't allow Dad to hurt me again.

We followed him through the maze of apartments and, even though I felt like he could protect me, I was also fearful my dad could jump out from behind a tree or the shadows at any time. We ended up on the street and I ran to Aunt Dianna, immediately beginning to cry. There were cop cars everywhere and multiple officers searching for my dad, who was still looking for me.

As I hugged Aunt Dianna, she said, "This will never happen to you again. The abuse is over, and everything will be OK from now on."

Suddenly, there was a commotion behind me. I turned around to look and, through the tears in my eyes, I saw Dad being handcuffed, his torso bent over the hood of the cop car.

Dad turned his head in my direction as they placed him in the police car. "You went ahead and did it now, boy. You feel good about putting your dad in jail, boy? I hope your friends are worth it."

My knees went weak, and a tornado of emotions ran through me as almost sixteen years of abuse came pouring out of my heart and soul. I wanted to run and wished my life could start over. I sobbed uncontrollably and was incredibly conflicted. On one hand, I felt horrible for putting Dad in jail. But, on the other hand, I felt like he was going to finally pay for the years of torture he put me through. Even though I couldn't start my life over, I could start it fresh from here.

The 6'5" officer walked back over to me after putting my dad in the cop car and knelt down to my eye level. He could tell I was in incredible emotional pain, so he softened his tone before he started speaking.

"Son, nobody deserves to be put through what you have and none of this is your fault. Your dad thinks he's a big tough guy, right? He's going to be just fine in jail. You let me deal with him."

The officer's words spoke right into my soul. Although I still cried, I began to regain my composure. My friends ran over to me and hugged me one last time before we left. They told me they were glad I ran and asked my aunt if they could see me again.

———

The ride home was quiet. It was nighttime and the city lights sparkled in the dark sky. I sat in silence, taking in the scenery and being alone in my thoughts. The windows were down. The car didn't have air conditioning and warm wind blew in my face, drying my tears. Aunt Dianna put her hand on my shoulder and told me she loved me. I felt like things were going to be better now. The armor I kept on to protect myself started to whittle away.

We arrived at Aunt Dianna's house, a small two-bedroom manufactured trailer with one bathroom. We pulled into the carport and walked towards the door.

She put her arm around me. "This is your house now. You are part of our family, and I won't ever let anything bad happen to you again."

Her husband, Rick, greeted us at the door. He had stayed back to watch my cousin, Brent. I enjoyed the time I spent with Rick. He always treated me so well and joked around with me. He knew this wasn't a good night to joke around.

"Welcome home, Walt. We're so glad you're going to live here. Everything's going to be OK. You're safe with us," Rick said.

"Thank you, it means a lot to me. I'm happy I'm moving in with you guys."

Brent ran up to me. He was only two-and-a-half years old and a ball of energy. Since Brent was an only child, I became like a big brother to him whenever we were together. He ran to the door and gave me a hug. The welcome I received gave me a glimmer of hope that everything was finally going to change. I felt like I was part of a happy family for the first time in my life. Although I wasn't their biological kid, I was thankful and blessed to be a part of their home.

As I lay in bed that night, a deep sense of calm rolled over my heart and soul like a fog over a field on a cold night. It seemed like it enveloped and covered the extreme turmoil I'd lived through. Finally, I wasn't worried about being woken up to get beat, berated, locked in a basement, moved to a new city, or any other type of abuse. I sensed the difference in my mind almost immediately. It felt like I hadn't slept in years. My level of exhaustion overwhelmed me. A lifetime of tension released as my body fell limp. My mind faded off into a dream of what my life would be like now that I was released from my prison, my lifetime of purgatory I didn't think I'd ever escape. I slept for fifteen hours straight until Aunt Dianna woke me up to make sure I was OK.

The next morning, Aunt Dianna made biscuits and gravy, my favorite breakfast. We talked throughout the morning about what social services expected to happen next, which would ultimately include testifying against my father in court.

Aunt Dianna reaffirmed, "You will never have to leave our home, regardless of anything your dad might do to try and retain custody. You will live here until you graduate from high school and become an adult." She placed her hand on my arm while she talked. She knew I would need to be taught how to accept a loving physical touch.

Rick also chimed in, " Nobody will ever come to our house and take you away. I won't ever allow it, so I don't want you to be concerned about that."

Happy tears streamed down my face. I felt so much love from them. "I'm so thankful for both of you. Thank you for helping me."

Aunt Dianna spent a lot of time with me when I moved in with them. She knew so many different things would manifest itself from the years of abuse I'd been through, and she wanted me to be intentional with how I handled myself.

The night Dad was arrested saved me from suicide or prison and changed the direction of my life forever. It is the single most important moment I've ever lived, even to this day. That night represented the beginning of my healing journey and a comeback continually evolving even to today. It wasn't an easy evolution. I still had years of growing, facing the pain of my abuse, letting go of anger, and learning how to receive love, but, without these events, I wouldn't be here to write this memoir. This catapulted my entire life and, ultimately, the legacy I will leave in this world into hyper drive.

The comeback starts now!

CHAPTER 12
FINDING MY VOICE

"Stop worrying about the price and just buy all the food," Aunt Dianna told me as we walked up and down the grocery store aisles.

I just looked at her and laughed. I have never known to have enough money to buy more than just a couple of things at once. When we passed the cookies, Aunt Dianna told me to grab a pack of my choice.

I immediately became uncomfortable. We didn't buy snacks growing up. I struggled to process that it was OK. "I'm fine. I don't need cookies."

She turned around and stopped the cart in the middle of the aisle.

"Everyone needs cookies and we're going to get some. So, you might as well get the ones you want."

She told me we received emergency food stamps from the state when I moved in, so it was fine, and I deserved them.

I picked the generic cream-filled sandwich cookies. "What about these? It's the same thing as the real ones and they're $2 cheaper."

She was really working hard to try and break my old habits. She took two bags of real Oreos off the shelf and set them into the cart.

"We're not going to buy those *because* they are $2 cheaper, son. We're going to get the name-brand ones. Since you're so worried about how much they cost, I'm going to buy two bags. You aren't going to have to worry about things like that anymore. I want you to enjoy being a teenager."

My brain worked overtime as she continued to put food into the cart. I felt anxious. I couldn't stop worrying about if we'd have enough money to pay for it all.

We finished the shopping trip. As we put everything on the belt, I told her, "I bet the total cost is $187.48."

She seemed a bit shocked but smiled. "Were you really calculating this whole time?"

"Yes, it's what I always do when I go to the store." I felt excited. This gave me a chance to show her how smart I was.

The cashier gave us the amount of $187.52. Aunt Dianna turned to me. "Wow, I'm really impressed with how brilliant you are! I can't believe you were only five cents off the total."

It felt great. She was the first person to ever tell me I was smart. It was also the most food I'd ever remembered buying at once. I found out years later it broke her heart that I had the hyper-vigilance and anxiousness of not having enough money so heavily ingrained into me that I'd calculated the amount so closely.

We loaded the groceries into the back of the car and jumped in. She grabbed a bag of Doritos and threw them in my lap so I could eat some on the way home. She told me I would never go hungry again. My heart was full as we drove home. I truly felt a sense of belonging for the first time in my life. I looked out the window of the car and put my hand out. I moved my hand up and down in the wind and felt the freedom of my new beginning.

———

The amount of gratitude I felt could've filled up an entire room. I was the happiest I'd ever been. We got to our small single wide trailer, and I unloaded the groceries while she put everything away and started dinner. Rick was also just getting home from his job delivering beer for Budweiser. He was in a great mood. I watched as he walked across the kitchen and gave Aunt Dianna a kiss before picking up Brent to give him a hug. He put his arm around my shoulders and said he'd help me get the rest of the groceries from the car.

We took a few trips back and forth from the trunk of the car. He pretended to juke past me every time, which made me crack up. Little moments like these really helped heal my heart.

It felt great to sit at a dinner table as a family that night. I especially loved getting to hear Aunt Dianna tell Rick how smart she thought I was for getting the total almost perfect earlier in the day. Rick told us about his day delivering beer and making giant displays at stores. I looked around to see happy smiling faces and thought, *Wow, somebody pinch me. Is this my new life?* Aunt Dianna made a great dinner. When we were done, I said I wanted to do the dishes. We all gathered the dishes from the table and put them into the sink together. Aunt Dianna told me she'd wash and I could dry and put the dishes away.

About halfway through the dishes, she grabbed the little sprayer next to the faucet and sprayed me with it. "Oh crap! I meant to rinse the dish off!"

She had a mischievous look on her face and sprayed me again. I grabbed some water in my hand and splashed her back. The water war had begun! It was so much fun. We both were soaked, even Brent got wet and splashed on the floor. It felt great to have such a good time. Aunt Dianna joyfully grabbed a mop and dried the floor, never once getting mad, while I finished putting away the dishes.

I grabbed one of the glasses with sunflowers and a yellow border unsure of where it went. I asked Aunt

Dianna and she pointed to a top cabinet, telling me to grab the stepladder next to the refrigerator so I could reach. I pulled the handle, opened up the door, and *crash!* The glass slipped out of my hand and broke on the floor.

I froze. She touched my arm. "Son, are you OK?"

I wasn't OK. I jumped as her hand came near me, instantly afraid she was going to smack and yell at me for breaking it. I tried to talk but stuttered and shook, which I did when I got nervous.

She grabbed my hand. "It's going to be OK. Seriously, it's just a glass. No big deal."

She had to help me down from the stepstool and walk me over to the couch. She sat next to me and hugged me until I stopped shaking. I felt awkward when people gave me a hug, but it also made me feel loved and warm inside. My mind flipped between pushing her away to allowing it. She turned on the TV and told me to watch basketball while she cleaned up the glass. I saw the tears and pain in her eyes as she glanced at me on the couch, my body still stiff from the fear. I hated that I couldn't control my physical and emotional reactions.

Dad got out of jail within a week and threatened my CPS caseworker. "I'm going to put you on *60 Minutes* for what you did to me."

The caseworker replied back, "Great, just make sure I know when so I can get my hair done first."

Dad called Aunt Dianna and threatened her, too. "You're going to pay for what you did. I'm getting custody of Walt back."

I overheard Aunt Dianna and Rick talking about how she would leave the city and move someplace to hide with me before she let me go back with him. I still had daily fear about my dad retaining custody of me. But, as the first month ended, I started to feel a lot more comfortable at their house and secure that I wouldn't have to go back with him.

I knew there was a massive hurdle to overcome. My day in court against Dad loomed large in my mind. Dad pleaded not guilty to abusing me and petitioned the court for a hearing. He told the court my friends and I lied about everything, and he wanted a chance to prove his innocence. All of us kids were then subpoenaed to court. I knew I was going to have to testify against him. I also knew it was my chance to have him held accountable. Even though I was terrified, I felt like it was something I had to do, which gave me the courage I needed.

The day finally arrived. I was going to testify and face my Dad, my abuser. I sat on the edge of the bed, getting my mind ready while I dressed. I pulled my new black dress slacks over my legs and took my time to button the white dress shirt, wishing I could delay the inevitable. I clipped on my red tie and finished putting gel in my hair, trying hard to look my best. I knew this was the biggest day of my life. The gravity of the outcome was all I could think about.

My emotions ran heavy as I mentally played out every possible scenario. I couldn't get the picture of Dad cross-examining me out of my head. I knew Dad chose to represent himself. He didn't have the money for an attorney. He also felt like he could do a better job. My mind juggled with protecting myself and wanting to protect my dad at the same time.

As we drove to the courthouse, Aunt Dianna told me again that there wasn't a chance she would let me go with Dad, regardless of what the court ruled. She attempted to reassure me that I would be OK, but I knew there was a possibility the court could decide to put me back with him. I didn't talk much. I couldn't find the words to say how I actually felt in the moment. We pulled into the courthouse parking lot and parked.

Before we got out of the car, Aunt Dianna told me to look at her. "I won't let them take you, even if we have to run away from the courthouse. I will be right in the front of the courtroom. If you get scared, don't look at anyone but me. I promise you I'm not going anywhere."

We entered the courtroom and stood in front of the judge. On the plaintiff's side was the state's attorney and me. On the defendant's side was just my Dad representing himself. My knees trembled and I felt weak when I made eye contact with him. My brain ran in a million different directions. All of my senses were on high alert. I wanted to run away, but knew I had to stand my ground.

The smell of oak filled my nose and the entire room. I tried to focus on the courtroom and not my emotions. The courtroom had light wooden paneling around the walls, chairs, and the judge's stand. The lights from the ceiling felt warm and beat down on me as I broke a sweat, mentally playing out the interrogation from Dad I knew was about to happen. The judge sat at a huge, elevated platform desk. Aunt Dianna sat in the front center and gave me a nod, letting me know it would be OK. Everyone's eyes fixated on me, the skinny sixteen-year-old kid ready to take on his abuser and who was scared as hell.

The bailiff announced the beginning of the proceedings. His voice boomed, "Please rise."

My legs felt like spaghetti. I used my hands to support myself on the desk in front of me.

The judge read the summons: "State of Arizona vs. Walter McKinley, Sr. for child abuse and endangerment."

My lawyer spoke next. He said that he was representing me. Then my father chimed in to say he was representing himself. I couldn't believe the next word out of Dad's mouth.

"Mr. McKinley, how do you plead?"

Dad sneered at me. "Not guilty."

I stood there in disbelief and wanted to scream out that he was a liar. The tension was palpable. I felt Dad's anger towards me as he stared my way during the lawyer's opening statement. My fear grew stronger, and my throat became extremely dry. I was petrified that he'd be found not guilty, even though we all knew the truth. The proceedings started and my father immediately asked the judge to separate all six of my friends and I.

Dad told the judge, "I want them separated because they are a bunch of liars. I want them watched the whole time so they can't talk to each other."

The judge agreed to the request and asked the bailiff to have a sheriff watch all of us in the waiting just outside the courtroom.

The judge looked at us as we lined up to leave the courtroom. "Please do not talk to each other while you are waiting. We will call you in one at a time to give your testimony. Do all of you understand?"

At fifteen and sixteen years old, we all understood the judge and the gravity of the situation. We nodded our heads in agreement. One by one, each of my friends were led into the courtroom when their name was called while the rest of us waited nervously outside. We made eye contact with each other, each of us slowly nodding our heads or opening our eyes wider to say "I got you" and "We have strength in numbers." We all knew the truth and I knew each of them was willing to do whatever it took to help me after the abuse they witnessed.

Dad asked them all the same question when they got on the stand. "What hand did I hit Walt with?"

Dad thought he could fool each one of them into saying his right hand because he was left-handed. He intended to use this to prove we were lying. Every one of my friends replayed the night in their heads. They sat on the witness stand and looked at their hands, imagining the positioning of my dad to make sure they gave the truest answer. All of them said it was the left hand, putting Dad on the defensive and causing him to change his course of action just as I was called into the courtroom for my testimony.

I felt everyone staring at me and I tried not to make eye contact. Dad's eyes burned a hole through my soul. His intimidating and peering look hit me right as I walked in. His head was slightly lowered, and he looked at me like a madman, attempting to strike fear into my heart. I looked towards the judge, attempting in my own way to regain my composure. The judge asked me to sit on his left side, in the witness stand.

The walk to the witness stand felt like an eternity. I tried to stay calm and strong on the outside. On the inside, I was terrified. I relived those moments when I was locked in a dark basement or beat into a ball in the corner of a room and felt like a scared little boy again. But I also had an inner strength propelling me through my fear and providing me the power to give my testimony.

"Walt, you are not in trouble. We're going to ask you a few questions and I want you to be honest. Nothing is going to happen to you. Just tell the truth and everything will be OK," the judge said as I sat down.

Looking at everyone in the courtroom, time moved at a snail's pace. I wiped the sweat off my forehead with my sleeve because my palms were too sweaty. I began to tap my foot against the platform and a groundswell of emotion started to take over me. I caught Dad's eyes and began to cry. I was mad and angry, but still felt horrible I was testifying against him.

The state attorney started to ask me questions about the night Dad hit me in front of my friends. I cleared my quivering voice. I couldn't stop looking over at Dad who still had a snarl on his face, the look of someone who would bury me in the desert if given the chance. I tried to refocus, but my mind went blank. I asked the lawyer if he could repeat the question. My eyes darted around the courtroom in a panicked state until my gaze caught Aunt Dianna's. She gave me a thumbs up and mouthed that it was OK. This was all I needed to start answering questions.

The state attorney did a tremendous job laying out the events of that night, but also telling the story of a boy who was tormented at the hands of his father and needed the state's protection to live a healthy life. He was meticulous and thorough. I answered the questions honestly and with conviction. Each time I answered and with every piece of my truth I told, I felt my confidence grow.

Dad had grown visibly frustrated. It was evident to everyone in the courtroom. I could tell he was ready to pounce when the judge turned the questioning over to him. It was one thing to answer questions from an attorney, but a whole other to answer questions from your abuser and father. I tried to keep my eyes fixed in Aunt Dianna's direction and gave short answers in bursts.

After fifteen minutes of questions meant to break me, I could feel my anger getting stronger towards him and the confidence that he would be held accountable growing by the second.

Dad asked me a question and I looked down, gathering my thoughts for a second until he snapped. "Look at me while I'm talking to you, boy!"

It was the same tone he'd use before beating me at home and the judge wasn't having it.

The judge immediately intervened. "If you talk to him like that again I'll hold you in contempt of court."

Dad tried to repeat questions in a different way, berating me in an attempt to fluster me into changing my answers. He worked hard to make it look like I wasn't telling the truth, but the difficulty of testifying against my father aside, I answered everything honestly.

As the questioning continued, my face flushed and my body warmed with adrenaline. Years of pent-up emotion and feelings of not being able to protect myself filled me with anger.

The tears were gone and replaced with rage as Dad intensified his questioning. "You're lying, boy. The truth will be told before we're done today."

I had enough! I wasn't taking this anymore. "You're lying! You know you did this to me; you've done things way worse than this. All you've ever done is beat on me and make me your slave."

I wished I could walk off the witness stand and punch him in the face. I was so angry. Breathing heavily, holding back angry tears, and leaning forward in my seat, I was ready to handle whatever questions were next. What happened next shocked me.

My reaction to Dad's questioning caused him to lose his temper and almost start yelling at me. "Who do you think you're talking to, boy?!"

The judge immediately cut him off. "That's enough! Mr. McKinley, if you treat your son this way in front of this entire courtroom and me, I can only imagine what you must be like behind closed doors. There will be no further questions. Walt, you can get down and go stand by your lawyer now. I've seen everything I need to. You did a great job."

Prior to reading the verdict, the judge said, "Walt, Jr., I believe everything you and your friends said today beyond a shadow of doubt, which makes my decision an easy one." He continued, "Mr. McKinley, I'm appalled by your behavior in my courtroom. No child should ever be treated the way you've treated your son. On the count of child abuse and child endangerment, the court finds the defendant Walter McKinley, Sr., guilty. I grant custody of Walter McKinley, Jr., to Dianna until the minor is eighteen years of age."

I felt vindicated as the judge read his guilty verdict and slammed his gavel on the bench, signifying the end of a lifetime of torture. I wanted to jump up and down in elation and relief. I lifted my eyes up. *I'm free. I'm free. I'm free.* It was one of the most powerful moments of my life.

I turned to look at Aunt Dianna who gave me the biggest smile. We both knew this meant I could stay with her for the rest of my teenage years. My abuse was officially over. Gone was the worry I'd be placed with Dad again. But the elation quickly turned back to pain as I looked at Dad being led away in handcuffs. I felt sad for him.

Dad looked at me. "I hope you're happy, boy." The judge cut in and told the bailiff to escort Dad from the courtroom immediately.

Once he was out of the courtroom, I felt the heavy weight of sixteen years of abuse lifted from my shoulders. The exhaustion of living in flight-or-fight-mode for my entire life hit me full force. I was finally allowed to walk to Aunt Dianna. Emotion uncontrollably poured out of me.

"It's finally over. I can't believe it's finally over."

"I know, honey. You're never going to go through anything like this again. You did amazing today and I'm so proud of how you stuck up for yourself on the stand."

"I'm really happy. This is a new chance for me, but I'm exhausted and just want to go home. I feel like I'm free for the first time in my life and I don't have to just survive anymore."

She put her arm around my shoulder as we walked out of the courtroom. "It's finally time to enjoy being a teenager and you don't have to worry about anything anymore!"

———

Life instantaneously became more normal than I'd ever experienced. The memory of testifying against my dad and all the years of abuse was still fresh but faded by the day. For the first time, I felt free from abuse and turmoil, secure that I wouldn't be tossed around like a baseball between homes and cities. The feeling I had was indescribable, but it's the highest level of gratitude and happiness someone can feel. I felt great!

I began my healing journey and quickly experienced incredible personal growth. My stuttering subsided as my fear dissipated and confidence grew. Aunt Dianna was my biggest cheerleader and I started to find what I loved about myself. The bondage of the pain from years of abuse was released as I spoke my truth. I was loved, celebrated, and told that I was an amazing person. It was what my heart and soul needed to jump start the rest of my life.

The county roads at night were pitch black. The dense fog rolled over the acres of lettuce fields like a protective layer between the ground and the cold air just above. Aunt Dianna, Brent, and I drove with the windows down, feeling the first big fall cold front roll in, extinguishing the last hot streak like a firefighter to an inferno.

Aunt Dianna shuddered. "I got a chill." She began rolling up her window.

"I got a chill. Take the wheel." Both of us laughed as I continued the rhyme.

"I got a chill, take the wheel, I'm cold for real," she said, continuing the game we were apparently now playing.

Hilarity ensued. We rhymed for another thirty minutes as we drove home, expounding on the rhyme each time, and laughing hysterically the entire way. This type of random fun was the norm in our house and had a dynamic changing effect on my personality.

We played music loud and had rap battles to our favorite songs. We'd shoot baskets on the basketball hoop outside and eat dinner together every night. For the first time in my life, I started talking about the future and felt true hope for its potential. I felt like a kid again, laughing and joking without a care in the world. The bond between all of us grew strong like the roots of an old oak tree, firmly planted and ready to weather any storm. I focused only on the good happening around me and buried the pain still sitting inside my chest into the deepest recesses of my being. I only wanted to allow happiness and joy to exude from me, but I still felt anger in the corners and dark places in my soul.

We were poor and didn't have much: a tiny single wide trailer, a car needing work, and minimal extra money. But the material things didn't matter. I felt truly loved for the first time in sixteen years.

I finished ninth grade at Kofa High School but had to transfer across town to Yuma High School for tenth grade so I could take the bus from Aunt Dianna's. Starting a new school was less intimidating this time. I was used to it after attending so many new schools. I'd become pretty adept at making new friends and, ultimately, nothing else mattered as long as I stayed with Aunt Dianna.

I had an intense desire to lift weights and build my skinny sixteen-year-old 130-pound frame to a point where I could protect myself and others. I also chose to join the basketball, cross-country, and track teams to acclimate me into the school and make friends. Sports and weights were a significant release for the pain I still carried. I focused my energy into every bench press, rebound, or mile I ran. These were outlets to positively channel my pain. I felt happy and was adjusting well. But I couldn't shake the undertone of resentment and frustration, just below the surface of my chest, I held towards my parents, Bruce, and childhood foster families. I became more impulsive and prone to exploding on other men. I felt a responsibility and desire to protect women and children.

Rick taught me how to drive in our little blue Toyota Corolla hatchback.

He told me it was best to learn on a stick-shift because "if you can drive a stick, then you can drive anything."

I didn't care what I learned on; driving was cathartic and freeing in a way nothing else was. I grinded the gears as we started down the street. The car jumped to a complete stop as I barely tapped on the gas. Rick chuckled and reassured me that it was totally normal. He told me to just restart the car and try again. I was thankful he didn't get pissed off at me burning up the clutch.

The car surged forward with a jolt, and we were off. Rick clapped his hands together in delight and slapped the dash, telling me he knew I could do it and that I was crushing it. The warmth hit my face through the window and my hair blew in the wind as he told me to push the clutch in and put it in second gear. The gravel road rumbled under my feet as the tires traversed over every rock. I felt alive and free!

We continued down the road until we hit an old, abandoned airstrip about three miles from the house. It was in rough shape from the sun beating down on the asphalt. Rick told me to floor it on the straightaway, so I pressed my foot against the gas pedal and heard the engine revving higher. I shifted into third gear, the exhilaration of the increasing speed overcoming the need to be careful, and a huge smile radiated from my face. Rick asked if I was ready. *Ready for what?* He pulled the emergency brake, and we spun in a circle. The tires squealed, my hands were in a white knuckled grip on the wheel, and my eyes bulged as I held on for dear life!

We slid to a stop. "One of the keys to driving is learning how to come out of a skid. Always turn your steering wheel *into* the skid, not with it." He grabbed the wheel and showed me what he meant. "We're going to try it again, OK?"

My racing heart was excited and nervous. I replayed turning into the skid over and over in my head while we picked up speed. I saw Rick reach for the emergency brake when we hit 35 miles an hour. We spun to the left. I turned the steering wheel to the right and, after a few seconds, I regained control of the car and we continued rolling straight down the runway.

"Wow! That was incredible!"

Rick let out a holler. "You did it on your first try, too. That was amazing, Walt!"

Little moments where I had a small victory and made someone proud of me did a lot for my self-worth and played a huge part in my healing.

———

A few months later, Aunt Dianna and Rick called me into the living room and said they needed to talk to me. Aunt Dianna patted the couch and told me to have a seat. Rick was sitting on a kitchen chair near the couch, and I could tell by their body language this wasn't going to be good news.

Aunt Dianna started the conversation. "Son, we need to talk to you about something. I don't want you to be scared because no matter what you are staying with me. Your Uncle Rick and I are getting a divorce."

I was stunned and didn't know what to say.

Aunt Dianna continued, "This is about us and has nothing to do with you or Brent. We love each other, but we just aren't *in* love anymore."

I began to cry. My new, happy family was breaking up. Even worse yet, I wondered what would happen to me.

I looked at both of them, beside myself at the news as they just shared with me. I knew they'd gotten aggravated with each other at times, but never guessed they were on the brink of divorce. My eyes welled up and I became emotional. I saw the tenderness in their faces and the care in their voices as they waited for me to respond.

"Do I have to go to a foster home or live with Dad?"

My stomach turned and my mind raced while I waited for what seemed like an eternity for their response. All of the bad memories flooded back, and my mind worked overtime, triaging every possible scenario in seconds. Aunt Dianna squared her body up to mine, grabbed my hand, and told me to look at her.

"I promise you will never live with anyone but me until you move out on your own. I don't care what we have to do, I will make sure it happens."

Rick also chimed in. "I'll be there to help support you guys and I'll help your aunt to make sure you stay with her."

Deep inside, I felt like the stress of being a teenager with so many issues, whose own parents didn't even want him, added to the tension in their marriage and, ultimately, their divorce.

Rick moved out and we stayed in our trailer. Aunt Dianna always exhibited a strong emotional exterior for Brent and me and constantly reassured me that I wasn't going anywhere unless we were together. Aunt Dianna, Brent, and I became like the Three Musketeers, going everywhere together and creating an unbreakable bond.

Aunt Dianna found a job working at a produce cooler after the divorce. It was long hours and a tough industry, especially for women. She worked her way up from running the scales weighing semi-trucks to being the general manager of the entire facility. We made her schedule work for our family and got help from family and friends to help run me around to sports activities.

Initially, we had even less money than before. But it still didn't matter. We had each other and love. Aunt Dianna bought a yellow Toyota in such rough shape that we had to turn off the engine if we were stopped, otherwise the smog would recirculate into the car and gas us out. Like most everything else, we found a way to laugh it off, even if it was embarrassing we had a smoke screen behind our car. We'd talk about this being only the beginning of an epic life adventure and dreamt about all the things we could achieve.

———

For Christmas that year, some of my family pitched in with my aunt and bought me a basketball hoop. Basketball was the ultimate outlet for me and became a challenging activity requiring my full concentration. When I played, I didn't think about all the things I'd been through, only how to crossover dribble or make another jump shot. I loved when Aunt Dianna would come out and shoot with me or would sometimes just be my cheering section from a chair under the carport. Brent even got into the fun. He was only three, but I'd lower the hoop and lift him up so he could practice dunking like Charles Barkley.

The next year was filled with all the normal things a teenager does in high school; Classes, sports, friends, and girls filled my days. I didn't have any contact with Dad, per the court order, and I liked it that way. It was great; I didn't need to try and manage a relationship with him or have the impact of seeing him while I was trying to regain traction and create positive life momentum. Aunt Dianna received a promotion at work, and we moved thirty minutes from the edge of the desert in the foothills of Yuma Arizona, into town where everything was much closer. Luckily, even though we were in a different school district, I got to finish my junior and senior years at Yuma High School.

Our house in Yuma was the second biggest house I'd ever lived in. I had my own room, and we even had our own pool. The best part of our new place was that it backed up to Kennedy Park where about twenty people played full-court basketball almost every night. Aunt Dianna would yell from the backyard for me to come home once it got late. Aunt Dianna, Brent, and I were our own little family unit and, even though she worked a lot of hours, we always made time to connect by telling jokes, eating together, or laughing about life.

Everybody knows everyone, especially if you grew up and stayed in a small town like Aunt Dianna did. She was the life of the party and would go hang out with friends at a local spot. I loved it because she'd bring people back to the house and we'd have huge parties. She was only nine years older than me and, at twenty-six years old, she was figuring out how to manage a family as a single mother and still have fun. People she worked with and other friends would come back to our house from the bar a couple times a month. It was every seventeen-year-old's dream and I enjoyed all the attention I received. There were pretty women around, all the guys she worked with were really cool, and sometimes I could even have a couple of beers.

There were a few times things got hectic and out of control at the parties, but I never cared because it was such a grand time. On one occasion, a big fight broke out between some of our closest friends and other guys who showed up looking for trouble. There were fists flying and people strewn all over the street in front of the house. It was getting chaotic, and police were called, but not before someone shot a handgun a couple of times into the air. A friend of our family ran into my bedroom and put his gun between my mattresses. Luckily, nobody was hurt. That night was hectic, but, generally, it was just a great time with people trying to have fun. Aunt Dianna said we weren't having any more parties at the house after the fight because it got too out of control and she didn't want to put us in that kind of danger.

Aunt Dianna created an environment where I could flourish and grow into my own person for those three and a half years I lived with her. Even with chaos sometimes happening around me, I always felt loved and safe. Life wasn't always perfect; sometimes we were broke, sometimes we had out-of-control parties, sometimes we were figuring out life on the fly—but it was all an important part of the journey.

I made it out of my purgatory and excelled against all odds in high school. I was able to do those things because I finally had someone who loved me, cheered for me, set healthy expectations, and kept me safe. My journey to healing still had bumpy roads once I moved out on my own. I still had a lot of unresolved anger. But Aunt Dianna gave my life positive momentum and a healthy foundation so I could launch myself forward.

CHAPTER 13

ADULTHOOD

After graduating from high school, I got a job for Pepsi Cola and started trying to create a life. Initially, I moved in with a friend, but he lost his apartment and I bounced around to a few places trying to save money. I wanted to forge my own path, and I didn't want to ask my family for help. I ended up living in my car with my friend, Robert, who was also trying to find a place. Luckily, Aunt Dianna was spending half the year in Salinas, California working in the produce industry and didn't realize I was living in my car. She would have been pissed at me for doing so. I would see my grandmother once a week and shower at her house when I was there, maintaining the facade that everything was going well so they wouldn't worry about me.

A few weeks after I started living in my car, I woke up and heard the beeping of a garbage truck right next to the spot where I parked. I was asleep in the driver's seat and Robert was asleep in the passenger seat. The crashing sound of the truck backing up startled me and was disorienting. The hydraulic noises and metal forks banged so close to me it seemed like someone was hitting pots and pans right next to my head.

I frantically looked around, still unable to fully open my eyes. My head was in a fog, pounding from the whiskey I'd drank the night before.

I hit Robert in his arm. "Wake up. This trash truck is picking up the car."

Robert jumped up in his seat, his eyes bulging out of their sockets. "Bro, what the heck are you talking about?"

I finally came to the realization that I was dreaming. The trash truck set down the large metal trash container next to us.

Robert laughed hysterically. "Oh man, I'm not ever letting you live this one down. This will be a joke forever!"

We broke out in laughter. "Bro, I legitimately thought the trash truck was picking us up in my sleep." We then got dressed and headed to work for the day.

We'd lived in my car for about a month. It was getting tiring, but both of us were too full of pride and we couldn't bring ourselves to ask for help.

One day, I put on my Pepsi shirt for work and turned to Robert. "We need to figure out new living arrangements."

He said he'd see if he could hustle some extra money by doing a few odd jobs since he wasn't working. I dropped him off near his parents' house and we agreed to meet at 6 pm at the Carl's Jr in the middle of town. I knew we had to do something. I couldn't take living in my car anymore.

Robert and I met once I finished my route. I was tired, hungry, and aggravated. The thought of sleeping in my car was really getting the best of me, especially with nighttime temperatures still hovering around 100 degrees. I knew this wasn't the kind of life I wanted to live.

I walked over to a payphone to call my grandmother for a visit. I missed her, but also knew I could shower, eat at her house, and spend some time in the air conditioning. I enjoyed Grandma's company and she took amazing care of me whenever I stopped by. She always had sage advice and was overjoyed when I visited. The time with her was extremely priceless. As the payphone rang, I saw a familiar face walking towards me.

Robert called out, "Bro, that's Morris. HEY, MORRIS!"

Morris turned to look in our direction. He was just as caught off guard and surprised as us. We hadn't seen each other since finishing high school almost a year earlier.

"Oh man, Walt and Robert! What the heck are you two doing?" Morris replied as he walked over to us.

"We're just working and living life. I stopped to give my grandma a call really quick, but how are you?"

"Where are you guys living?" Morris asked.

"A few different places," Robert said.

Morris walked towards my car and could see the back seat full of our clothes. "It looks like you're living in your car, Walt. I have two extra empty rooms in a four-bedroom house. If you guys want to rent the two rooms, I can talk to my roommate, Abby, and see if she's cool about it."

It took Robert and I about one second to respond. Opportunities like this didn't come along every day. I was grateful. The timing couldn't have been more perfect. Morris went inside the store to buy beer for all three of us and we followed him back to his house. We spent the rest of the night drinking and catching up on what we'd been up to over the last year.

Morris was on the chubby side, had long hair, and wore glasses. Although he was Hispanic, he didn't speak any Spanish. He had a hippy vibe and was always in a great mood with a smile on his face. His joy was palpable; the kind of joy that makes you smile no matter what's happening around you. When we got back to the house, he introduced us to his roommate, Abby. She was about the same height as Morris. Between their physical attributes, and easy-going attitudes, they seemed like brother and sister.

It seemed like a great fit between the four of us right off the bat. It worked out perfectly. They had two people who would pay rent, and we had a place to call home without breaking the bank. I unloaded my stuff from my car and flopped down on the bed in the room, ecstatic I didn't have to sleep upright in the driver seat anymore. It was truly a blessing!

Morris told us after that high school he had a chance to work at a Christian bookstore close to his house and he'd met Abby at the church's young adult group. Abby was looking for roommates since her parents left her the house and because it was so large. She needed help with upkeep. I cut Morris off and jokingly said he didn't strike me as someone who'd work at a Christian bookstore or go to young adult groups, especially since he drank and smoked a lot of weed.

He made a smoke ring while exhaling the weed. "Jesus made plants and marijuana, so why shouldn't I enjoy it? He made it for people just like me."

We all broke out in laughter and carried the night away telling stories about how far we'd come and pontificating on what our futures still held.

———

We settled into living with them quickly. I couldn't get over the joy emanating from Morris every day. I had happy days, but I spent most of my time with an undertone of anger. The pain I repressed while living with Aunt Dianna was real and manifesting itself in unhealthy ways. I was still protective of those I felt couldn't protect themselves and was hyper aggressive towards any man who dared to look my way. I loathed feeling this resentment and despair and needed to find a release so it wouldn't hold me back anymore. I just didn't know how to let go of sixteen years of intense abuse and the feelings of wanting to hurt my abusers.

Over a few beers, I told Morris and Abby I was angry at the world and, if given the chance, I'd bury the people who hurt me.

"I know what you need, bro. Why don't you come to the church's young adult group with us tomorrow night? It's a great opportunity to meet new people, plus it helped me let go of things from my childhood eating me up inside. I think it could do the same for you," Morris said.

I felt immediately compelled to go and told him I was in. I thought if he was so happy because of church all the time, then I wanted a piece of it, too. I was lost and felt anything giving my life purpose and meaning was worth the time. I didn't want to wear the mask of happiness anymore. I wanted to actually be happy instead.

We walked into the Catholic chapel and I immediately felt uncomfortable, especially since I'd only set foot in a church maybe five times in my entire life. Directly in the front was a twenty-foot crucifix with Jesus hanging from it. I felt like he was looking right down at me. Beautiful multi-colored stain-glass windows shone brightly as the large ceiling lights reflected off of them. The sanctuary felt enormous. The ceilings were three stories high and the pews were in rows running from the very back all the way to the altar.

Morris blessed himself with holy water when we walked in. I followed suit, not wanting to look stupid in front of everyone. Immediately, I felt emotional standing in the back, looking up at Jesus.

Morris turned around. "Let's go to the front. We'll all sit together."

The youth pastor talked and joked around with other young adults in the front. My soul was stirred, and I felt a familiar presence in church. I recalled my grandma taking me here a few times when I was younger. I remembered being so rambunctious that I could hardly sit still. It was boring at the time and I couldn't wait to leave.

This time I felt different. All the other people came up and gave us a hug while introducing themselves to me and Robert. They were glowing, loving life, and talking about normal things young adults do like going to school, where they worked, and what parties were happening. I felt at ease because they included me in the conversation and talked about topics I was comfortable with.

We sat down in the back and the youth pastor started his sermon. He read a passage from the Bible and began to correlate it to the struggles of being a young adult. He talked about being quick to anger, feelings of wanting to hurt others, and finding forgiveness for what's happened in our lives. I felt like a little boy again, antsy and ready to leave. At that moment, I felt like he was talking directly to me. Once he finished talking, the pastor asked all of us to break off into smaller groups. He reminded everyone to sit with people we didn't know, to talk about emotions we struggled with, and to give the pain over to God.

Even though I was there with Robert and Morris, I felt alone and on an island. Robert and Morris were more spiritual than me and I didn't know how to act or share, so I planned on just being quiet. I was petrified. I felt the emotion swirl just inside my chest, and I didn't want anyone to see me cry. A group of five people asked me to join them. One of the men talked about how he was abused and how he struggled to find forgiveness, which kept him in an angry state of mind. The sweat on my palms started to build. I could relate to everything he said. I wanted to share and release the pain but didn't know where to even start.

He asked me if I wanted to share next. My brain raced at a million miles an hour. *Do I say something? Should I make something up? How do I tell them about what really happened to me? Would they think I was weird, or would my story scare them? Even worse, would they even care?*

It seemed like an eternity as I just looked at them and processed my thoughts. I felt like I wanted to clam up and not say anything, but also felt like I had to let the pain go. I told them I felt the pastor was talking directly to me the entire sermon and it was like he could see into my soul. I told them how I wanted to do better, but also how I had an uncontrollable urge to hurt other men. That it was almost like an evil force took me over when I'd get angry.

One person in my group spoke up. "That's God talking to you through the Pastor, Walt, and those feelings you're having are God trying to reach you. What happened to you?"

Normally my defense mechanism in situations like these was to act tough. I was taught men don't cry and to bite my upper lip, but I couldn't hold it back any longer. I talked about how I was physically and emotionally abused by every adult I'd known until I was almost sixteen. My chin quivered and my eyes welled up with tears. I tried as hard as I could to talk, but the emotions overtook me like a tsunami does on the shoreline—coming in hard, fast and full of unstoppable energy.

I broke down in tears and the group all put their hands on me to pray for God to give me peace and healing. I tried to control my emotions and was embarrassed. But I also felt a freedom from finally talking about my story with others. It was like I was letting go of my deepest and darkest secrets. The pastor closed us out in prayer, and we all said our goodbyes before leaving.

I turned to walk out of the chapel and felt a pull to approach the altar. I'd never prayed before, but I couldn't deny the feeling and needed to go up to the stairs. It was like my legs had a mind of their own. Morris and Robert followed me to the altar, and we all hit our knees to pray at the feet of Jesus. Paralyzed with deep soul-filled pain, and not knowing how this worked, I tried to talk to God. The burden in my heart was heavy and my voice cracked as I began to speak. I cried out, "God, please help me." I had so much to say but I couldn't speak any other words. I broke down in tears, sobbing like a baby. Each tear felt like it cleansed me and flowed out of me like a river trying to wash away the pain in my soul.

Morris prayed over us as I continued to cry. The pain inside of me was so deep and personal. God was the only one who knew how I truly felt inside. The fake joy and tough façade were stripped away as my battered heart and soul were left on display for all to see. My vulnerability was fully in the open for the first time in my life, and I didn't care. I wanted to feel better, and I was ready to figure out how. I took in a long, deep breath. It was the kind of breath you take when you feel suffocated underwater and come up for your first gasping breath of air. God breathed life into me that day and opened up my spirit to his healing powers.

My tears suddenly stopped as quickly as they had begun. I felt the difference down to the core of my humanity. I felt weightless and almost hovered back to my feet. God removed the heavy backpack I'd carried around my entire life and left it on the altar. It's hard to explain, but it was the purest, most uplifting, moment I'd ever felt at that point in my life. The spring in my step was noticeable to everyone watching as I walked past the pews and out the door. I was giddy and laughing. The emotion of the moment was incredibly cathartic and drew me closer to God.

We walked past another separate building with a more intimate area to pray. I told Morris and Robert I'd like to go in for a bit. I sat down in silence and began to pray, but this time I didn't cry and the emotion felt different. This was a personal conversation between me and God. I asked him to take my pain, to help me find the right path, to guide me, and to help me have a family to love one day. I didn't realize it then, but I gave my life over to Jesus that day.

Those intimate moments, and the euphoric feeling after, became something I've never forgotten, even in my darkest hours. I knew there would still be some dark and challenging times ahead. I knew the conflict between good and evil still whirled like a tornado through my mind, body, and soul. I didn't change and become healed overnight, but it was another profound step in finding salvation.

———

Living with Morris turned out to be a huge blessing for us, but it didn't mean we were doing the right thing all the time. Morris and Robert smoked weed in the backyard almost every day and always tried to get me to do it with them. I didn't care if they smoked it, but I was against doing it myself. I was extraordinarily focused on not becoming my parents but found myself chasing easy highs and turning my attention to women, partying, and fighting as my life spiraled out of control. I battled the internal demons telling me to do the easy and fun thing while trying to keep from straying too far off the path.

One day, Morris jokingly asked me for the hundredth time to smoke a bowl of weed. Most times it was a quick "hell no" followed by laughter from all of us. On this particular day, I didn't care anymore. I'd been around it all my life and wanted to see what the big deal was. I told them I would do it, only if they never asked me again. They looked at me, stunned. Then Robert took off running down the street to buy a $20 bag of weed. He sprinted back into the house after about five minutes. I could tell both of them were excited I was actually willing to smoke with them this time.

I still wasn't quite sure I would do it. But I thought, *What the hell? Let's see what all the buzz is about.* Robert and Morris pulled out a white five-gallon bucket from under a bench in the backyard and filled it up with water. They coached me through how to take a gravity hit, which basically meant taking a two-liter bottle full of smoke into your lungs at once. Morris pushed the two-liter down in the water, forcing the smoke into his lungs then holding it in for a few seconds before exhaling a giant plume of smoke into the air.

I hated the skunk smell of weed. It seemed to linger on forever and permeated every fabric of clothing on your body. But it was my turn! I was committed and knew there was no turning back, regardless of how I felt about it. They filled the two-liter bottle back up with smoke. I put my lips around the opening at the top and pushed the bottle towards the water, inhaling the smoke as I did. The smoke entirely filled my lungs. The pressure was intense. I let the smoke out and immediately went into a coughing frenzy. Both of them laughed hysterically. I couldn't stop coughing. Each time my lungs flexed, it felt like I re-inhaled whatever was making me cough, creating a never-ending cycle until I almost threw up.

I looked towards them both. Their squinty eyes and girlish giggles were hilarious.

"You feel it, Walt?" Robert asked.

"Hell no, I don't feel it. This is a total disappointment because I don't feel anything except for this stupid cough!" I replied.

I couldn't believe I finally relented only to be left without any effect. They told me that you don't typically get high on your first time you don't get high. This was a bummer. They definitely oversold and under delivered the outcome.

We lived with Morris a few more months before Robert and I moved into an apartment after Abby's parents sold the house we were living in.

My life continued to spiral out of control. The moment I'd experienced in church became a far-off memory. I spent days working for Pepsi and partying at night. Drinking with friends and chasing girls was the norm and I found my body could run off three to four hours of sleep a night. The alcohol and girls seemed to fill a void in my life; a need to be wanted and loved in a way I didn't feel worthy of. I didn't like being alone, so I tried to surround myself with people at all times.

I tiptoed on the line of being responsible by going to work during the week, and being irresponsible by drinking heavily every weekend. I was the life of the party; loud, boisterous, and acting like I didn't care what anyone thought. But, inside, I was still a broken and unfulfilled soul. When I was drunk, I was able to cut loose and escape the mental purgatory that still haunted me. I craved being around others because it gave me energy, but it really kept me from being alone with my thoughts and insecurities. I had a mean streak that was untamable when pushed, like a demon inside of me keeping me on the brink of uncontrollable rage.

One day, we kept hearing a car honking its horn across the street, waking us up from a drunken slumber from the night before. It was early for a Saturday and the honking was incessant.

Robert screamed out from our second-story apartment. "Go in the fucking house and stop honking the horn! Stop being fucking lazy!" One of the men who lived there stepped out of the house.

The man yelled back, "Why don't you come over here and make me?"

I flew off the couch and to the window. I was instantly triggered. I wasn't going to let someone talk to us like that and I definitely wasn't going to get punked out by some random guy across the street. I jumped out the window and landed two floors down in the dirt and grass. I was barefoot and wore basketball shorts with a white T-shirt. Jumping from so high hurt my feet. I didn't care. All I saw was red. Robert jumped out of the window right behind me just as ready to fight.

The guy across the street was our age. He ran back inside his house to get his brother. Anger had a way of taking my mind over and intensely triggering me to a point where I wanted to unleash real pain on whoever caused it.

Both of the men ran back out of the house. I yelled loudly, "The best thing for you right now is to get back in your house before your blood ends up on the concrete!"

They tried to act tough, but I could sense their fear and it made me feel strong and powerful. After being oppressed my whole life, it felt good to know I could strike fear into someone else. I had the power now and I wasn't willing to relinquish it.

A friend ran out to the front of the apartment complex carrying a pellet gun. It looked like a real gun and the two guys immediately went back into their house. My adrenaline was pumping, and I was ready to hurt them. Ultimately, I was glad it didn't end in a physical altercation because I was terrified of unleashing my pent-up pain. Back in the apartment, I cracked a beer and tried to extinguish the fire still fueling my body, trying anything to release the negative energy.

The next six months were filled with so much drinking, partying, and trips to Mexican clubs to fill a lifetime. My spirit shifted for the worse, but another life changing pivotal moment was about to take place.

Although I still worked, money was scarce and the idea to rob a store sprang up during a drunken bender after we'd just spent our last dollars to buy more alcohol. Spiraling out of control and struggling to get myself back on track, I thought about the spoils from robbing a store and not the potential of going to prison if we got caught. The internal battle between good and evil was real as I toiled between being a good-hearted man, and an angry young adult who felt the world owed me for all the years of abuse. I felt empty inside and no amount of girls or alcohol was ever enough to substitute the pain.

Robert and I made a plan to rob a Circle K convenience store. It was on a side street with multiple getaway options. Robert and I knew when only one older man worked and figured he wouldn't resist us. We cased the store and attempted to learn the nuances of the cash drawer, how many customers came in early in the morning, and where the security cameras were located.

I walked into the store about 11 pm a few weeks before our robbery and talked to the frail, old man working behind the counter. I looked clean cut and had a knack for striking up a conversation, so he told me everything I wanted to know. Through our conversation, I found out the best day and time, where the cameras were located, and if he'd put up resistance if robbed. It was go time!

Robert and I calculated and prepared for every part of the robbery; guns, ski masks, car, even how to grab the surveillance tape from the back office. No detail was spared. We agreed ahead of time that under no circumstances would we hurt the old guy. As long as he was compliant, we would only tie up his wrists and nothing else. We did, however, talk about making sure he opened the black safe under the cash register where most of the big bills were.

Wednesday night between 2 and 3 am was our target time. This was when the least amount of people were on the roads. We had the entire robbery perfectly laid out, but we didn't plan for divine intervention to interrupt our course of action.

The Monday before the robbery, we were making final preparations and ensuring we had even the smallest details covered. Then the phone rang. Robert picked up the phone and I saw his entire body language change. His voice became frantic. I could tell whatever he heard wasn't good, especially when he stood up before ending the call and grabbed a bag for clothes.

Robert got off the phone and told me he had to find a ride to his mother's house three hours away. She was deathly ill. We knew my car couldn't make the five-hour drive without breaking down so Robert decided to hitchhike. I drove him to the Love's Travel Stop right next to the freeway so he could hitch a ride. Robert called me later and told me he made it to his mom's house in time and she made a full recovery. God intervened for two punk kids who needed saving from a potential robbery. Without her being sick, we probably would've ended up in prison.

———

Life was crazy, chaotic, and tumultuous. I had so many people around all the time, so I really never spent time alone until the week after Robert left for his mom's. I sat in the apartment alone with my thoughts and the pain of my childhood over the next few days. I reflected on what I'd been through and where I was going. I thought about the plan to rob the Circle K and how idiotic it was. I couldn't believe I was really going to go through with it and how easy it felt for me to do so. The reality that we could really hurt someone or even go to prison made me pause long enough to reassess my life direction. I made a decision to get out of Yuma that night, regardless of what it took to make it happen.

I drove to my grandma's house the next day. I needed her wisdom. I took the long way through county roads, reflecting about what I was going to do and how I could change the direction I was headed. I got to her house, and she could tell I was off right away. She always had a sixth sense for her grandkids. I could tell I held a special place in her heart ever since I was three and she saved me from my foster mom.

She grabbed me an iced tea. "Let's go sit on the screened porch and catch up."

The wicker furniture and green turf were nostalgic. It brought back great memories of our time and talks together. Those great memories brought me peace but seemed far off in the distance compared to the ones that haunted me daily.

I told Grandma I wasn't in a good place and really struggling to make the right decisions. It was almost like an angel was on one shoulder and devil on the other, both chirping in my ear at all times.

Grandma told me, "In life, we have choices, grandson, and those choices can affect the course of the next fifty years. It's time for you to do what all my boys did at your age. It's time for you to serve our country in the military. There is nothing good coming for you if you stay in Yuma."

"You're right, Grandma. If I don't get out of here, I don't know what the heck is going to happen. I need to do something."

She reached her hand over and placed it on mine. Her hands were aged but held the strength of a thousand lifetimes. "Stay for dinner and in the spare room for the night." She said the Lord's prayer and asked for God to give me strength and wisdom to start a new life.

Grandma woke me up early to watch the sunrise with her. She had a sense of humor, just like me, so she woke me up like it was my first day in the military. We laughed and gave each other a hard time all the way through breakfast. I never doubted Grandma's love or purity of wisdom and I believed she knew just what I needed to do.

After sleeping on it for the night, I felt resolute that joining the military was the right decision. It would provide me with the most options for the future. Grandma's brown ornate cuckoo clock clicked, and the bird shot out from the top. It cuckooed eight times. 8 am, our time to head to the military recruiter station.

My grandfather and uncle served in the Navy, so I thought that would be a good place to start. I spent the summer after I graduated high school in Washington with my uncle. He wove tales of visiting amazing places around the world, which seemed really cool to me. He had a good life and plenty of money to take care of his family, so I figured going into the military could give me a lot of what I wanted.

I walked in and told the Navy recruiter that my grandfather and uncle served and I wanted to follow in their footsteps. I told him I wanted to be an officer, a pilot, or a Navy Seal. I knew my goals were as audacious as my attitude, but I wanted success. Success was my chance to get as far away from my childhood as possible. Success was something I felt I could control, and I knew I was a hard worker.

The recruiter stood up and shook my hand. He was gregarious and a big man, standing about six inches taller than me. He looked like a war hero from where I stood. His pristinely pressed white uniform, shiny black shoes, and eighteen ribbons were impressive.

He sat back down and leaned forward in his chair. "Well, son, those are some challenging goals. If you don't have a degree, there are ways to be an officer in the Navy, but it doesn't come without hard work and a little bit of luck. If you want to be a Navy Seal, you can try and pass the physical fitness test while in boot camp, so I suggest you get really good at pushups."

"As long as there is a chance, I want to sign up. How do I make it happen?"

I knew I needed to get out of Yuma to have a better life, and I knew my grandmother was waiting outside for me to say I was enlisting, so I pressed forward with my plan.

I met the recruiter back at the station the following Monday. I was excited and nervous for the new adventure. We drove 45 minutes away to the recruiting station in a nearby town so I could take the ASVAB test. I took the test and they graded it on the spot. The recruiter walked out and said I scored very high then showed me specific jobs I was qualified for and discussed the pros and cons with me.

He told me spots in boot camp were available now and I could leave as soon as possible. It was a quick decision and turnaround on when I'd leave, but I just wanted to move forward. Aunt Dianna was still in Salinas running a produce cooler and I knew there was a possibility I couldn't say goodbye. I ultimately chose to leave two weeks later, knowing the longer I stayed in Yuma the more likely I was to change my mind. Luckily, I got to say goodbye to Aunt Dianna and thank her for helping turn me into a man.

It was time for me to change my legacy and the lineage of my future children. I knew this was the first real commitment, and step, to ensuring abuse would be eradicated from my family forever. I was all in and ready to take the reins of my life like never before.

CHAPTER 14
THE NAVY

Leaving Yuma was freeing in a way I never expected. No longer was I reminded of the many places I lived and was tormented. I stopped looking in the rear-view mirror of life and started focusing on the windshield. It was cathartic and invigorating. I knew this was a unique opportunity to create a version of myself I always wanted. Nobody would know me, or my past, and my life could literally be anything I wanted it to be. It was the first time in my life I was free to be my authentic self.

The eight hours of travel and plane flights from San Diego to Chicago was a perfect opportunity for me to reset. I spent the flight dreaming about the future, my career, my future family, and a life free from torment. I couldn't help but smile the entire flight and felt like my life was finally going in the direction I'd envisioned since I was eight. My life was on a new adventure with limitless possibilities, and I felt like a million bucks.

The transfer bus from the airport to boot camp pulled up to the large double black gates at the Navy Recruit Training Command in Great Lakes, Illinois. Two sailors in their dress blues and white Dixie-cup hats talked to the driver then opened the gates. I felt my heart beating and nervousness growing with each passing second. For a moment, I thought, *Holy crap. What did I do?* But I shook it off and looked out the window, mentally preparing to start Navy boot camp.

The drill instructors were waiting for us to get off the bus and started yelling immediately.

Multiple drill instructors were in our face at the same time yelling, "Move! Move! Move! Get over there! Move your ass! Why are you so slow?!" Everything was in overdrive, and I felt the crisp Great Lakes air cold on my face. I was initially warped back to a stuttering, nervous, and scared kid as the strong coffee smell on the drill instructor's breath smacked me right in the face, his nose hovering only a centimeter from my cheek.

Almost instantaneously, my timidness turned to anger. *Who the fuck is he talking to?*

He pushed my shoulder forward towards the other running recruits heading towards the building where we'd get checked in for our sixty-day "staycation." "Run, recruit!"

I hustled towards the line of over 100 recruits and saw the drill instructors continuing to yell at everyone, systematically breaking all of us down before building us back up. I knew I needed to quickly check my emotions and not take the yelling and intimidation so personally. It was part of the process and would be my reality for the next two months. I made a decision to control my reactions any time one of them invaded my personal space. It was one of the first times I was able to purposely keep a calm response. I learned a valuable lesson on how intentional actions could create a non-reactive emotional response.

We got to the payphones and were allowed to make a two minute collect call to our families so that they knew we arrived safely. I called Aunt Dianna. She picked up right away. Two minutes went by extremely quick, so we talked as fast as possible, attempting to get every word out.

"I hate you're gone, but I'm really proud of you."

"I love you and will call you the next time I can. Give Brent and Grandma a hug from me," I told her.

A drill instructor walked between the recruits on the phones. The echo of his voice rang out clearly. "Two minutes is up. Get back in line. We're going to the barracks, ladies."

We walked across the base and passed other divisions of sailors all marching in precise lockstep with each other, like a perfect dance. Military cadences, which kept the eighty sailors marching in unison, rang out like a harmonic chorus.

It was like a different world compared to Arizona. Gone was the sandy hot desert, replaced instead by grass, trees, and cold wind from the Great Lakes. I felt invigorated and hopeful this was the life changer I was hoping it would be.

———

The daily screaming and yelling in our faces became the norm as the drill instructors tested our ability to handle stress and take direction when under pressure. The synergy built between eighty men stuffed in open-bay barracks and sharing toilets, food, homesick emotions, and daily physical fitness beatdowns created an unshakable camaraderie that solidified our military indoctrination.

The last week of boot camp, our drill instructor played, and had us sing, "God Bless the USA" by Lee Greenwood. It was emotional. There wasn't a dry eye. Singing the chorus, "I'm proud to be an American," felt different now. It held a new reverence, and my purpose was, for the first time, something greater than myself. I was now serving our country and protecting freedom around the world.

The pride I felt on graduation day was beyond anything I'd ever experienced. For two months, we'd been mentally and physically exhausted and simultaneously lifted back up to be strong representatives of our amazing country. We lined up outside the graduation building on an extremely cold but bright blue skied November morning. The Navy band played and I watched the last few families walk into the building.

"Forward, march!" our drill instructor ordered.

We entered the building. The band hit the first notes of "Anchors Aweigh," the Navy's hymn. 400 graduating sailors sang in unison. The sound was deafening.

Stand Navy out to sea, fight our battle cry!

We'll never change our course so vicious foes steer shy-y-y-y...

Newly minted sailors marched around the indoor track in our pristinely pressed dress blue Cracker Jack uniform, shined shoes, and brand-new white Dixie-cup covers. The building was packed with people, full of families with huge proud smiles and fluttering hearts of joy. I knew I accomplished something done by so few in our country. I made it, and the sky truly was the limit. I felt in control of the next phase of my life, and I was determined to make it extraordinary.

Between the military, twenty-year-old testosterone, and the pain I didn't realize I was still holding onto, I had a huge chip on my shoulder. It protected me and masked the years of abuse and subsequent inadequacy I still felt. At times, I was conflicted and filled with self-doubt. My past still haunted my dreams, and I could hear my abusers telling me I wasn't good enough or that I'd never amount to anything. But I also heard Aunt Dianna telling me I could do anything I set my mind to and that I was special. On the outside, I was strong, confident, and fun. But on the inside, I was frantically searching for joy and trying to be in control of everything happening around me.

It was a late November Friday night when I arrived at my first duty station, a submarine base in Groton, Connecticut. Snow was on the ground, and it was so cold outside I could see my breath in the van lights. I stepped out of the van and looked at the eight-story building that was going to be my home for the next year. I checked in at the quarterdeck just inside the entrance and was given a key on the fourth floor.

I made my way down the hall and up the elevator. The crème-colored cinder block walls of the barracks looked extremely well built, like they were able to withstand a nuclear blast. Once out of the elevator, I passed a common area with a bunch of sailors drinking and playing spades. I was still in my dress blues so they could tell I was straight from bootcamp.

"Hey Shipmate, drop your stuff in your room and come have a drink with us," one of them called to me.

Their friendliness caught me a little off guard. "Sure, I'll be right back out."

I opened the door to my room and heard Tupac Shakur playing from a radio. My new roommate looked up from his book and asked if I was moving in. I confirmed I was and walked over to the twin bed across the room to set my sea bag down. He stood up and introduced himself as Townsend and we shook hands. I could tell he was from Louisiana because of his accent.

I told Townsend I was going to go grab a beer with the others in the lounge area and invited him to join.

The sailors in the lounge shared stories about working in the fleet, port visits during deployments, and how they enjoyed Navy life. This type of family atmosphere is what I hoped the military would be like. It was refreshing to live it firsthand.

The next morning, I woke up early because I was excited to see the entire base. The base housed a good portion of the Navy's fast attack submarines on the East Coast and also all of the submarine schools, which is what I was going to attend. Since I didn't have a car yet, I walked to the Navy exchange to buy some normal civilian clothes. Mountains, trees, windy roads, and submarines lined the shoreline, giving the base a unique feel. The color of the leaves was magnificent. The trees were in full fall change. Vibrant yellows, oranges, and reds covered every branch.

The base was a self-contained city with everything you needed to eat, sleep, and work on one giant swath of land. I took a deep breath in and picked up some snow. It felt like I was a kid in a candy store as I walked down the hill and towards the exchange to buy everything I needed for my new life.

Life began settling in as I built a routine of attending submarine school during the week, working out and playing basketball every night, and hanging out with my new friends. We'd party and have a few drinks on the weekend. But I knew that if I wanted a different outcome for my life, I had to truly be different now.

With so much more to lose, I focused on specific goals for my career and held myself accountable to controlling my drinking and anger. I spent a lot of time studying at the schoolhouse so I would get priority selection over my duty station after school was over. I committed to not drinking any alcohol during the week, only on the weekends. I also worked on not taking things so personal. I knew people weren't always trying to test me and had to remind myself not to fight someone when they got under my skin.

Even though I shored up a lot of my behaviors, the exciting and pulse-racing appeal of meeting women filled my veins like a drug that fed my insatiable appetite for affection and acceptance. I tried to fill the gaping hole in my heart. I focused on making friends with women at nearby colleges, the base club, and local parties. Little did I know I would soon meet the love of my life—my soulmate—and the woman who would show me an entirely different side of myself.

The first night I met her, my friend Nick and I's plans were diverted because he got sick from eating pizza. We had planned to drive to Club Caesars, the eighteen and older club at the University of Rhode Island. My mind was set on having some fun for the night, so I walked to the base club. I would not be denied some fun. Typically, the base club didn't have a good ratio of women to men because it was on the submarine base, but it was a great place to hang out in a pinch and I knew some of my other friends would be there.

I walked up the stairs and into black lights lighting the entire room. Multi-colored carousel lights sprinkled colors all over the walls. The strobe lights made the mobbed dance floor look like people were flashing. The music pounded, the bass hit my chest as Notorious B.I.G. played through the club's loudspeakers. I noticed a group of my friends and headed in their direction.

I'd always try to walk in with swagger, attempting to make people notice me. My body moved and my head bobbed up and down as I cut my way through the crowd. We'd all been drinking earlier in the barracks, and I was feeling pretty good.

I put my hands out wide and yelled, "What's up, fellas? It's time to party!"

They all dabbed me up and gave me a dude hug. The night was young, the club was jumping, and we were living our best lives. Hyped song after song came on, building the excitement in the club. The dance floor was broken up into two sections separating the upper level from the lower. It was packed.

I saw a group of women out of the corner of my eye dancing on the upper level and I couldn't help but notice one in particular.

She was beautiful. Her long curly brown hair, almond shaped brown eyes, and smile mesmerized me from across the bar. She wore a long sleeve white striped shirt, a pair of boots, and tight flare jeans that fit her perfectly. I knew, with so many other men in the club, that I needed to shoot my shot and I needed to do it now.

I walked through the crowd, carving a path towards her. Self-doubt built as I approached her, but my newfound confidence battled it back.

I walked up behind her and lightly grabbed her side, attempting to get her attention. She and her friends were ducking under the rail on the second floor and moving to the bottom dance floor. She looked back—I swear right at me—and followed her friends. I saw my buddies laughing over on the side, and I knew I had to try again or I would never hear the end of it.

I took a breath. *I got this.* I walked around and down the three steps to the bottom. Her back was turned to me, so I tapped her on her shoulder. She turned around and I smiled as big as I could. The gap between my teeth, dad made fun of me about, was filled only 2 months earlier. Having it closed up gave me the confidence to show my giant smile and personality.

She turned around and I said, "Hey, I was trying to get your attention up there. My name is Walt. What is your name?"

She flashed her smile at me. "Oh, sorry, I didn't see you. I'm Stephanie."

"Nice to meet you. Do you want to dance?"

She said yes right away. The pitter-patter of my heart, the ego boost, and the feeling of acceptance filled me like an overflowing cup. We danced the night away and spent hours talking about who we were, where we came from, and what we liked. It was amazing. We were comfortable with each other like we'd been friends for years.

I asked for her number as the night came to a close, trying to be cool and attempting to leave a little mystery by leaving before the last few songs. She wrote it on a napkin and I stuck it in my pocket. I told her I'd give her a call in a couple of days. My walk back to the barracks that night had a distinctly different feel. I had a hop in my step as I imagined taking this amazing and beautiful woman out on our first date.

A few days later, I was practicing for the base basketball league playoffs and dislocated my ankle while rebounding a shot during a pick-up game. It was gruesome and required an immediate ambulance ride to the base hospital. Since it only dislocated, and didn't break, the rehabilitation time was more extensive. My ligaments were stretched significantly prior to my ankle being popped back into place. I called Stephanie a few days later and apologized for my delay. Even though I really wanted to take her one a date, it would have to wait. God's blessings come in ways that aren't visible until you look back on life's path. This was one of those blessings.

Stephanie and I talked every night for the next month as my ankle healed enough to go on our first date. I really liked her and was getting impatient to see her again. We were quickly finding our compatibility was off the charts and our chemistry was on fire.

I was about a week away from getting my cast off and couldn't wait any longer. We decided to double date so she would feel the most comfortable, and I needed someone to drive since I was still in a cast.

I nervously crutched up the front door of her yellow house. Her house had dark shutters and a half circle driveway surrounded by trees. It seemed like something out of a hallmark movie to me.

Her dad answered the door and I introduced myself. "Hi, sir, my name is Walt. I'm here to pick up Stephanie."

"Hi Walt, my name is George. Stephanie didn't tell me you would be on crutches."

I couldn't help but chuckle at his comment. He probably thought I was crazy to go on a first date while on crutches. He invited us in to meet her mother and we talked to them for a few minutes before our dates came down the stairs.

Stephanie took my breath away. She looked beautiful in her shimmery silver shirt and jeans. She was just like I remembered. My heart leapt out of my chest as she walked down the stairs and looked at me. The connection we'd created on the phone the last four weeks was solidified in that moment. I thanked her parents for their hospitality and we headed out. I loved how supportive and loving they all seemed and knew I wanted to come back to visit again.

We drove to Rhode Island. Stephanie sat with me in the back seat and we held hands while the four of us talked the entire way. We pulled up to the Outback Steakhouse and walked in, well I crutched in anyway.

I joked as Stephanie grabbed the door for me. "This is a role reversal." Internally, I was embarrassed that she had to hold the door. I tried to bolster my confidence a bit. *It doesn't matter if you're on crutches. C'mon, Walt, pull it together.*

We sat down at the table. My ankle was swollen and pulsating from accidentally losing my balance getting off the tall bar stools we were waiting on moments before. Luckily, Stephanie didn't see me cringe in pain. I tried to pull her chair out the best I could and set my crutches against the wall next to us as I sat in the chair next to her.

BAM! The crutches slid down the wall and hit the floor with a loud thud.

I closed my eyes. *Oh man, this date is not going well. So much for being Mr. Smooth!*

I made a joke at my own expense to divert the gasps coming from everyone around us as my buddy picked up the crutches. The rest of dinner went great, and we headed to a comedy club.

Even though I was on crutches and feeling clumsy, the chemistry between me and Stephanie was undeniable. It came so easily. Even though our relationship was new, it fit like a glove. The rest of the night was filled with laughs and a goodnight kiss I'll always remember. It was electric. I felt on top of the world on the drive home from her house. Nick and I talked the entire way about how well the dates went. He commented how it seemed like Stephanie and I knew each other for years.

She was my soulmate and I knew it.

———

The next year and a half went by extremely quick. Stephanie and I were in love and submarine school was coming to a close. I'd worked extraordinarily hard to ensure I ranked in the top of my class so I would get my choice of orders. Ranking near the top would give me the best possibility to stay in Connecticut, close to Stephanie while she went to college at the University of Rhode Island. I didn't want anything to derail my relationship with her. She completed who I was and made me a better person. Stephanie was the yin to my yang. I couldn't imagine my life without her.

Our class instructor, Chief Petty Officer Smith, called my roommate, Matt, and I into the office at the Submarine school. I was a bit apprehensive. I felt everyone's eyes turn and look at us as we walked in the room. There was a feeling in the air of disappointing news and I could tell that everyone felt bad about what was coming.

My mind raced. *Did I do something wrong? No, I haven't done anything. Why are they staring at us?*

Chief Smith was one of my favorite instructors. He was an impeccable example of who we could become and he really cared about his sailors.

"Well, men, I'm sorry to say that both of your military orders to stay at the submarine base in Connecticut are revoked. Unfortunately, the needs of the Navy take precedence and there are greater needs in other places right now. One of you is going to Hawaii and one of you is going to Norfolk, Virginia."

My heart dropped. Disappointment and rage immediately boiled inside of me. I'd had enough setbacks in life. This wasn't fair. I tried to maintain my composure as I took a few seconds to collect my thoughts before responding.

What am I going to do? Stephanie and I were ecstatic to continue our relationship. Getting orders to Groton would allow me to stay close to her. How would we make it work if I was forced to move?

I felt pissed off and frustrated. I'd worked extremely hard against some brilliant people to earn second in the class and get a premium pick at location.

"Petty Officer McKinley, you're going to Hawaii."

What the fuck? You aren't even giving us a choice? "Is there flexibility on where we go as long as we fill the two billets? Chief, can you give Matt and I the weekend to discuss it?"

"As long as the two billets get filled, it doesn't matter where you go. You have until Monday, but I need an answer early."

"Dude, I'll take your Hawaii orders if you want. I know you and Stephanie are really serious. I've always wanted to go to Hawaii, so I prefer it anyway. Either way, I'll do whatever you decide. Let me know after you talk to her," Matt said.

I drove over to Stephanie's house that night after work and told her I had some pivotal and life changing news.

She looked at me with wide eyes. "What does that mean?"

She felt my disappointment. I saw the look of concern hit her face as I gathered my thoughts. I didn't want to lose her, and I emotionally prepared myself to hear her answer.

"Well, they told me today there are no longer orders for Connecticut and gave me the choice between Hawaii and Virginia for my next duty station. There isn't anything I can do about it, either. I was told that the needs of the Navy trump any chance I have of staying."

She sunk into the couch and looked like she'd been punched in the gut. She turned to me. "Where do you want to go?"

"Well, I love you and want to give us a real chance at being together for forever. I will pick Virginia if you'll move with me. But if you don't, or feel like you can't go, I'm going to choose Hawaii." Deep down, we both knew a long-distance relationship wouldn't work.

If we were going to stay together, we'd have to move together.

"Wow, I didn't expect this. It's a big decision. I'm already set up to transfer from the community college to the University of Rhode Island in a few months. All my grants and loans are set and I'm even getting a dorm room. I love you, but I need some time to think about it."

"I understand. Take the weekend to think about it. Either way, I have to give my decision first thing Monday morning. I'll give you some space tomorrow and come back Sunday afternoon so we can discuss what you want to do."

She cried and we hugged each other on the couch. We both understood the gravity of this life-altering decision. Either way, it was a monumental change. I just wanted to keep us together. Even though Stephanie didn't realize how significant of an impact she was making on me, she was helping heal my heart and soul.

———

I left for her house mid-morning on Sunday. The drive felt much longer than normal. The winding tree-lined roads normally made for speeding around were pivot points for my racing mind, playing every scenario of her decision in my mind with every turn.

I hope she comes with me. I'm going to be devastated if she doesn't go. We can start an amazing life together. I don't know what I'm going to do. My mind changed from amazing to terrible outcomes like the flip of a switch, doubt creeping in as I inched closer to her house.

I played the mixtape she made me for a birthday gift. Our song, "Always and Forever" by Luther Vandross, started to play. I hadn't prayed since I was nineteen and in the church, balling my eyes out. But in this moment, I prayed to God to put the wheels in motion and help us find a way to be together. I couldn't stand the thought of not having her in my life. I had enough taken away from me in my lifetime. She made my cup overflow with joy like nothing else ever could.

I crept into her driveway. The dirt crunched under the tires, cracking loudly as I slowly moved around the U-shape and into my normal parking spot behind her dad's car. She stood outside on the porch waiting for me. She flashed her beautiful smile and gave me a hug. She seemed happy, so I allowed hope to take the place of the fear I was feeling.

I was flooded with emotion and tried to keep it together. *How am I so lucky to be loved by such an amazing person? God, I'm counting on you.*

We walked over to her room in silence, hand in hand, both of us knowing the importance of the conversation about to happen.

We sat on her bed and faced each other. "I've been doing a lot of thinking about what the right decision is, and if I should move. I can't shake the feeling in my heart that moving with you is 100% the right decision. I know my parents are probably going to be upset, but they will always be there for me. I love you and I don't want to ever look back on my life and wonder what if I moved, what if I had made the decision to go. I can always come back home and go to school here. My parents are always going to be there for me, but I don't know if I'll ever have the love we do again. I want to move to Virginia because I still want to be able to visit with my family, which would be much harder from Hawaii. If you can get orders there, I'm in."

I put my head back, closed my eyes, and thanked God. I wanted to run through the house and outside screaming in elation. It was one of the most joyful and relief filled moments of my life.

We hugged each other. "I love you, too, and am so happy we're going to take this leap together. I'll let Chief know that I'll take the order to Virginia tomorrow. I can't promise you that things will always be perfect, but I can promise to love and protect you as long as I'm still breathing."

I'd never felt so happy in my entire life. This was the another real step to creating the life I'd dreamt about, a life with a wife and kids full of happiness, amazing adventures, memories, and family traditions. I was on the top of the world!

CHAPTER 15
SUBMARINES

I left for Virginia four months earlier than Stephanie and reported to the USS Jacksonville, a fast attack nuclear submarine. I needed to get settled into my new job and find us a place to live before the end of summer. Since we weren't married, I knew it would be a tougher task because money was tight. Stephanie worked two jobs during the summer to buy a car and save money for the move.

The submarine was much smaller in person than I expected. Its long, black tube and topside sail was my new home for the foreseeable future. Its 130 sailors my new family. Walking down the pier, I felt the anticipation and excitement. This was what I was waiting for. It was time to protect my country in a much bigger way.

I walked past the guard shack and saw the giant blue banner with yellow lettering "USS Jacksonville (SSN-699)" on the bow. I showed the topside watch my orders and went down the ladder into the submarine.

The air had just a tinge of gasoline smell that permeated the entire space. The passageways were so narrow that we had to turn and walk sideways past other sailors.

I was greeted by the Chief Petty Officer who brought me into the wardroom to meet the Weapons, Executive, and Commanding Officers. With only 130 sailors on the submarine, it felt like a tight knit family. I couldn't wait to make my mark on it.

I hit the ground running the only way I knew how—by working hard. The primary job when first getting to the sub was starting and finishing qualifications as quickly as possible. I knew getting qualification on a submarine and earning your "Dolphins" was a hard task (typically took most submariners twelve to eighteen months to achieve). I had no intent on taking that long.

I knew I had four months until Stephanie came to Virginia, so I set out on a breakneck pace to achieve the qualification. I told Leading Petty Officer Grady that I wanted to achieve the goal in four months and asked his advice on how I could do it.

He gave a hearty laugh as he set down multiple three-inch-thick books. He said I'd need to study these and describe them in enough detail to each department so that they'd endorse my knowledge. "Good luck. The record is six months. I don't even know how you'd get close in four because it's so much information. I love your tenacity already, Petty Officer McKinley."

———

After almost three months onboard, the Chief Corpsman called me in to tell me there were red flags in my medical record and asked why I was diagnosed with reactive airway disease.

"In Connecticut, I got sick because of the massive change of weather and new allergies. I was wheezing and struggling to breathe, so I went to the medical department. After a few tests, the doctor told me that I had reactive airway disease."

"You need to schedule an appointment to meet with the pulmonologist at the Naval hospital and get medically cleared before we leave for a thirty-day sea trial in two weeks. If you can't get cleared, I can't allow you to go."

This better not stop me from going out to sea. It was the last barrier to getting my warfare qualifications, the prestigious Dolphins. I went to the pulmonology appointment like I was directed and was told the doctor would administer a test called the methacholine challenge. The results would unequivocally determine if I had asthma.

I had to breathe medicine in through a tube, which, if I had the condition, would induce an asthma attack. In only a bit of time, the results were definitive: I had asthma, a non-negotiable disqualifier for any submariner. I was devastated. I just spent almost two years in school preparing for this job and I had a great reputation onboard the submarine. I felt like my Naval career was being derailed before it even started. It just didn't seem fair, after everything I'd been through, for me to have another setback.

Stephanie was arriving in two weeks and I didn't know what I was going to do. *How the hell would I take care of her if the Navy decided to medically discharge me?* I had one chance; a medical review board was going to determine if I was qualified for other roles in the Navy. This was my potential saving grace and opportunity to continue my career. I embarked on a plan to eliminate anything I couldn't control. I was hell-bent on working towards creating an amazing life with Stephanie and was willing to do whatever it took to reach the goal.

I reported to the Submarine Squadron Support Unit in Norfolk while the Navy determined my fitness for continued duty. This duty station introduced me to the first man I ever accepted mentorship from. His name is Corey and he changed my life forever. We are still friends to this day. Our first interaction was hilarious and a microcosm of the shit-talking that happens in the military.

I walked into the office, knocked on the door jam, and bellowed out, "Petty Officer McKinley, reporting for duty!"

Four enlisted sailors and two officers turned their chairs in unison and seemed surprised.

The leading Petty Officer, and my new boss, Corey, turned around. "Cut that shit out. No need for that here. C'mon in."

Corey is a 5'7" African American man with a personality the size of a giant, and a heart of gold to match. He is a champion for his people and invests his energy in making those around him better. He loves giving people a hard time and expects one in return. It is his way of bonding and it fits right in line with my personality. We became quick friends.

He looked right at me and, without flinching, said, "Damn, you got a big ass nose."

Awkward silence fell over the room. Even though he caught me a little by surprise, I knew just what to reply. "Well, at least it isn't as big as yours, so I must be OK."

Everyone in the office let out a huge laugh. Corey stood up and shook my hand.

He slapped me on the shoulder. "That was hilarious! Finally someone who can match me! With a sense of humor like that, you're going to fit in well here. You're sitting right here next to me."

Corey became my first real professional mentor, and it couldn't have come at a better time. He helped me grow as a leader but, more importantly, as a man. He was an extremely hard worker and understood how to navigate office politics while remaining true to himself. He and his wife welcomed Stephanie and I with open arms, helping make the transition to our new life more fruitful. I am who I am because of the effort he put into me while we worked together.

———

Over the next year, I watched and learned how to operate within a team and find success. Corey taught me the chip on my shoulder wouldn't do me, or anyone else, any good. He knew my goals and told me he would show me how to achieve them. He had audacious goals, too, and our ambition deeply connected us. I trusted Corey. I opened up about my life and found out that we shared many similarities. It felt good to know I wasn't alone.

"In life, there's a game being played. It doesn't matter if you agree or not, the reality is that it's happening. You can either play the game or get played. There is no in between. You're smart enough to play it, now you just need to decide to," he told me often.

He helped me understand the value of personal connections and being true to my authentic self. I enrolled in night school on the base with the end goal of earning a commission and becoming a Naval Officer—a goal I wanted to achieve since I joined the Navy. I'd work all day and take night college classes on the base. I used tuition assistance so I wouldn't accrue debt, just like Corey taught me. Stephanie was a blessing and extremely supportive of my goal. She shared the vision for our future and worked as hard as I did. We were both willing to make sacrifices, even if it meant a little less time for us in those moments.

Corey and I spent time talking about our hopes and dreams.

"You're wasting your talent and you're way too smart for the Navy," Corey would often tell me.

He believed I was destined to change the world and saw potential I didn't see in myself. It was hard for me to trust people. I still hung onto the unresolved pain and the fear of getting hurt. But he earned my lifelong trust in those twelve months we served together. It's a friendship we still maintain today.

Eighteen months after I was disqualified from submarines, the Navy's Bureau of Medicine (BUMED), sent a final determination on my continued service. The results came with little fanfare and were stuffed in a manila envelope given to me from the mailroom. My hands shook as I realized what it was. This was it! This was going to determine my career and new direction for my life.

I had an impeccable reputation at my command and loved serving in the military. It gave me purpose, kept me out of trouble, and helped me take care of Stephanie. My mind went in every direction possible before I opened the envelope. Sometimes I hated that my mind thought this way. I knew it was from living in chaos my whole life and it was impossible for me to stop my mind from thinking this way and, honestly, I didn't try to prevent it. In some ways, it allowed me control over my next steps, something I was denied as a child.

I put my head back and closed my eyes, praying to God I didn't get kicked out of the Navy for asthma. I slowly looked down and flipped the paperwork over to read the verdict.

"Petty Officer McKinley, the Bureau of Naval Medicine determines you are eligible to retain your Naval service but are hereby disqualified from submarines, effective immediately."

I was disappointed that I couldn't be on submarines, but thankful I wasn't going to be medically discharged.

I continued to take college courses at night and shifted my focus on getting enough college credits to apply for the Enlisted Commissioning Program. I'd worked extremely hard over the course of my tour and taken on the most difficult roles. I was focused on showing my worth and continuing to excel even amongst the turmoil surrounding the next steps in my career. All of the dedication and focus was about to pay off.

My Commanding Officer called me to his office and asked me to sit down. He had a presence about him, one inspiring loyalty and trust. It was something I fully respected and wanted to learn how to exemplify. He told me that, after careful consideration, I was selected as Junior Sailor of the Year. I was so excited! It felt like electricity was running through my veins! This was something on my goal list and I knew I earned it. I felt professionally accomplished for the first time. The emotion was insatiable. I wanted to replicate the feeling over and over again.

———

With Junior Sailor of the Year, a 3.8 GPA, my Associates degree, and incredible endorsements from senior leaders in my organization, I had what I needed to be ultra-competitive for the Enlisted Commissioning Program. So, I officially applied. The only thing left to do was wait for a few months for the decision. While I waited, I was told I needed to pick a new job since I couldn't be a Fire Control Technician on submarines anymore.

I knew I could pick almost any role I wanted so I took time to decide what offered me the best opportunities in and out of the Navy. Making sure I was set up for jobs when I transitioned out of the military was also an important factor in my decision. I decided I wanted to go into the intelligence field as an Intelligence Specialist. I envisioned scenes from James Bond or Jack Ryan. The school was in our town, which meant I didn't have to be away from Stephanie. It was a win-win.

I transferred to a temporary unit for a couple of months until school started. It didn't require me to be at work every day, so I decided to pick up a second job waiting tables at the Olive Garden to help Stephanie and I furnish our apartment. We had used and hand-me-down basics to start, but I felt she deserved nicer furnishings and wanted to make sure I did whatever I could to get them for her.

Stephanie worked mostly in the evenings at Walmart. So, I picked up a few evening shifts a week, too. Working at Olive Garden was a blast. I enjoyed interacting with customers, meeting new friends, and making a lot of money. I knew the financial gain was the push we needed to kickstart our new life together.

During intelligence school, Stephanie's parents came down to visit and see our apartment. I was happy to see her so excited. Stephanie and I talked about getting married and I knew this was my opportunity to ask her Dad's permission. If I was going to change my family legacy, I needed to start our engagement off the right way. Asking her father was a crucial moment.

George and I sat on the couch, watching the Los Angeles Chargers football game. It was just the two of us. We finally had the chance to be alone. We both loved sports, and he had also served in the Navy, so conversation between us was always easy. At one point, the game hit a lull. I knew this was my time to ask the big question. I cleared my throat and nervousness filled my body.

I knew I needed to stop overthinking and just go for it. "George, you know how much Stephanie and I love each other. I want to spend the rest of my life making her happy. I have a lot of respect for you and Mary Ellen, so I wanted to ask for your permission and blessing to marry her."

Whew! I said it. Five seconds felt like 500 minutes as we looked at each other.

"I know you guys love each other and you make my daughter happy. You don't need my permission, but you definitely have my blessing."

"Thank you! That means a lot." There was an awkward pause. Neither of us knew what to say.

Just then, Phillip Rivers threw a beautiful touchdown to Antonio Gates for a Chargers score. We both celebrated the amazing play and were glad it broke the awkward silence.

———

Stephanie and I started planning our wedding, working hard to figure out where we would have it. Stephanie's family was in Connecticut and Pennsylvania and mine were all in Arizona. We knew since neither of us came from money we'd need to keep it on a budget, so we settled on Virginia Beach.

A few weeks later and towards the end of the intelligence course, we finally got my orders. I had a sickening feeling it wasn't going to be where I wanted to go and that I'd be sent to Bahrain or Japan. We weren't allowed to pick orders like in submarine school. We were just given them based upon the needs of the Navy.

My anticipation was high while the class instructor read out our last name and where we were going. Everyone was hoping they'd get one of their top three locations. I felt the same.

Finally, it was my turn. "McKinley, USS Kittyhawk, Yokosuka, Japan," the instructor announced.

My blood boiled. *What the heck? That was one of the places I didn't want to go!*

I talked to the instructor at the end of the day to see if I could change my orders, to one of my top three pics, but was told that the new command needed an E-4 and I was the only one in the class with that rank. The orders were non-negotiable.

I was sick of the setbacks continuing to haunt me. But since I'd started healing my past and talking about what happened to me, I was in more control of my emotions, so I refrained from losing my cool. I refused to allow a change of course to destroy my life. I was determined to make the best of my situation.

I drove back to our apartment and sat Stephanie down to tell her the bad news. It was especially bad because we couldn't move with each other until we were married. We already set the wheels of getting married in motion, but only had a four-week timeline to act before I transferred. We knew we needed to act quickly so she could be added to the orders and move with me. So, we eloped.

The situation wasn't ideal for either of us, especially for her. She wanted the fairy tale experience of family, friends, the white dress, makeup, and all of the other amazing things a traditional wedding offered. But we knew that, ultimately, getting married was what both of us wanted. If we had each other, we had everything.

We were married on July 3, 1999 by a Justice of the Peace on a hot and muggy summer day. She looked more beautiful than ever. She was my real-life queen and we've lived happily ever after since.

Then the day came for me to leave for Japan. I was still waiting on results of the officer program so we decided I'd go to Japan by myself and let Stephanie finish the school year at Old Dominion University.

Stephanie dropped me off at the airport. She was crying. It would be several months before we'd see each other again. Spending time apart was somewhat easier before because we had monthly visits. This time would be different; I would literally be a half a world away. I felt terrible leaving my newly married wife on the other side of the planet while I left to defend freedom and democracy, but also knew I had a mission to complete.

She hugged me tighter than she ever had. We said our goodbyes and I boarded the flight. I looked out the passenger window and saw her looking towards the

Boeing 747. With 500 people onboard, I didn't know if she'd see me waving and blowing her a kiss out of my window seat, but she did. She pressed her hand against the glass, and I could see tears running down her face.

I spent most of the seventeen-hour flight feeling like I'd let her down. I tried to logically rectify that we'd made the right decision. If everything went as planned, I'd be back in four months to attend college through the Enlisted Commissioning Program, and we'd be together again.

CHAPTER 16

SETBACKS AND COMEBACKS

I arrived at USS Kitty-Hawk, which, at the time, was the Navy's oldest ship and aircraft carrier. It was much more different than the submarine. The aircraft carrier was the size of the pier. The smell of gas, grease, and fumes filled my nose as I walked down the pier to report for duty.

Man, the Kitty-Hawk is huge. It feels about the size of the Empire State building.

I looked up in awe of the engineering marvel in front of me. The excitement of a brand-new adventure overcame the nervousness of starting all over again. I also had a sense of pride knowing that my grandfather had served onboard the USS Kitty-Hawk during Vietnam.

"Well, Walt, this is your new home," I said to myself.

I knew, with over 5,500 sailors and ninety aircraft, it would take some getting used to. Adjusting my seabag, I climbed the mountain of steps leading to the quarterdeck. Once I got to the top, I told the watch stander I was reporting to the Intelligence Center onboard and he called for someone to come get me.

We climbed three more levels before hitting the O3 level where the Intelligence Center—called the CVIC—was located. My section of the ship had blue tiles that indicated, unless on official business, enlisted sailors had to walk around to get to other parts of the ship.

My Leading Petty Officer, IS1, introduced me to the other two sailors on duty for the night. They were required to staff CVIC for twenty-four-hour stretches on the weekend, so I knew they'd be in the center all night. I was thankful there was someone I could talk to. The ship was like a ghost town because all the other sailors left for the weekend.

IS1 told me to follow him to my bunk in the intelligence berthing area. I followed closely behind and tried to pay attention to the direction we were headed so I could get back to CVIC when we were done. The ship was huge and had multiple passageways going every direction. We went down seven flights of stairs and entered the eighty-man berthing. Bunks called coffin lockers, stacked three high, lined the entirety of the compartment. It was just enough space for one person to stand between the six bunks per cube.

I grabbed the empty middle bunk and started to put my stuff away. I lifted the entire bed and put the bar in the front to prop it up. I carefully folded and rolled my clothes to ensure I could get everything inside. The space for our clothes and any extra items was extremely small.

No wonder they call these things coffin lockers. I think coffins have more space than this.

IS1 left for the evening. After I'd finished putting my clothes in my bunk, I decided to go back up to CVIC.

Left became right and up became down as I attempted to backtrack my steps to the CVIC. The ship was empty and everyone who wasn't on watch was long gone for the weekend. I really needed to ask someone where the blue tiles were, but there wasn't a soul in sight, so I kept looking.

I walked up and down ladders, port to starboard, and fore to aft looking for the blue tiles. It was more than thirty minutes before I finally stumbled onto them as I passed through a thick blue curtain. I recognized the "Officer Country" sign and knew I was almost there.

I was starving. I happily jumped at the opportunity to pitch in when my new shipmates told me they were ordering pizza. They both told me about their first weeks and how many times they got lost trying to find their way around. This made me feel better about my fiasco. The beauty about the military is that we're all new every few years, so 99.9% of sailors are welcoming. We create families with those we serve with.

My new friends taught me how to use the Navy's switchboard operator to connect to Stephanie back in Norfolk. Talking to her soothed my soul and gave me peace, and reminded me what I was fighting for. We talked for the next few hours about how much we missed each other and how four months should go by quickly. I couldn't use the phone line every day, but between the switchboard and paid calling cards, we talked at least five days a week. I was lonely and hearing her voice spoke straight to my heart and helped alleviate my insecurities.

A month later, I received official word that I'd been selected for the Enlisted Commissioning Program. I'd be heading back to Virginia to finish college with Stephanie in the fall. I was over the moon and grateful that we only had a couple of months until we'd be together. I'd achieved such an important professional milestone of being the first military officer in my family. I knew how much of a game changer being an officer was to our future. The weeks quickly turned into months. I shifted my focus from leading my division to returning back home.

I was promoted to E-5 and earned Sailor of the Quarter just before leaving the ship. I had an insatiable appetite to always be the best. I felt like each milestone and winning moment took me as far away from my childhood as possible and kept me ultra-motivated. Little did I know that I was fast approaching another obstacle.

A few weeks before I was supposed to return back home, I received a letter from BUMED telling me that I was disqualified from the officer program because of my asthma. "Petty Officer McKinley, we regret to inform you that your acceptance into the ECP program is revoked immediately due to asthma conditions that make you non-worldwide deployable."

I sat in shock, not saying a word. The rage of a lifetime of setbacks flooded my brain and emotions. Every time I felt like my life was headed in a positive direction, I was knocked back with a massive disappointment. I was pissed and hurt about the program, but also devastated that Stephanie and I had just spent the last four months apart only to be told I wasn't worldwide deployable. I picked up a book and threw it across the Intelligence Center. It slammed into the giant satellite imagery machine and next to my division officer's head.

"Damn it, I can't believe this! What do these assholes mean I'm not worldwide deployable? I'm in freaking Japan!" I screamed.

My outburst caused everyone to turn their head in my direction. Tears of rage filled my eyes as the feeling of disappointment continued to flood my entire being. I was more unstable emotionally then I'd felt in years. My division officer knew right away. He pulled me into the sound insulated compartment meant for only the most top-secret information to talk. I gave him the letter and he read it.

He put his hand on my shoulder. "This is bullshit, but you need to calm down. You are an amazing sailor and a vital part of our leadership team. We'll work with the doctors to try and get a waiver for you."

The Commanding Officer, Medical Officer, and I called BUMED and talked to the head of the medical approval process for officer selection boards.

"I don't understand how I'm disqualified under the pretext of not being worldwide deployable when I'm stationed in Japan. It doesn't get more worldwide."

The BUMED representative said, "Based on current officer billets and the Navy shrinking its total staff, we cannot waive asthmatic conditions, even if you pass medical tests. I'm sorry, Petty Officer McKinley, but you're not eligible to proceed with the program."

I was dejected and my knee jerk reaction was to get out of the Navy immediately. After being disqualified from submarines and now the Enlisted Commissioning program, I just wanted to transition back to the civilian world. I was triggered and acting irrationally about how to get out of my remaining 4 year obligation.

I met with the Commanding Officer of the ship and he told me, "You are an incredibly valuable member of the team and one of the top sailors on the ship. I understand how frustrated you must be but stay the course. What can I do to keep you focused on the future?"

"I need my wife to be able to join me in Japan. I still have two and a half years on this tour. Being apart that long won't work for either of us."

"I'll do whatever it takes to make it happen. Don't even worry about that."

I took leave once all the documentation for Stephanie's move was completed and headed to get her. I boarded the plane and flew back to the United States on a mission; I was going to get my wife! We'd been apart for eight long months at this point, and I wasn't willing to be away from her any longer. She picked me up in the airport and it was one of the happiest moments of my life. We were reunited and it felt amazing. I stepped off the plane and we both ran towards each other, embracing in a ten-minute hug. She flew back with me, and we moved temporarily into the Navy Lodge until housing became available. We didn't know our entire life was about to shift.

———

On September 11, 2001, we turned off our movie in the Navy Lodge and prepared for bed. What looked like a Bruce Willis movie played on the muted TV. The North Twin Tower was smoking and in flames. It took me a few moments to realize that this wasn't a movie. I glanced back and saw a news anchor come on the screen. I unmuted the TV. He said that a plane crashed into the North Twin Tower in New York City.

Stephanie sat next to me on the edge of the bed, just in time to see the second plane hit the South Tower. The anchor came back on to say a third plane was hijacked and that America was under attack.

My adrenaline spiked! I knew I needed to do something but wasn't sure what.

I looked at Stephanie. "I'm probably going to get recalled to the ship. If America is under attack, then we have to retaliate. I won't deploy without being able to come back to the Navy Lodge to help you get home, but expect we're going to war. I will make 100% sure you get home to your parents' house."

The phone rang and I knew what the call was. Stephanie held my hand as I picked up the receiver. "Petty Officer McKinley, all personnel are recalled to their commands immediately. Report for duty ASAP."

I hung up the phone. "It's going to be OK. I'll be able to call you from the ship. You know where the galley and exchange are so you can get something to eat on base. You'll be safe here. I'll keep you informed as I hear more. I have to go."

We hugged and kissed goodbye, both of us not entirely sure what was coming.

A couple of days later, the ship's medical officer called me into his office. It was his job to ensure everyone on the ship was physically ready for deployment. My medical disqualification from the officer program months beforehand put a red flag on my record.

"Petty Officer McKinley, when the ship leaves in two days you're staying on shore. We've determined that, since you aren't worldwide deployable as an officer, then you aren't enlisted, either."

As a sailor, I was heartbroken. I was ready to retaliate for terrorists attacking our great country. I was ready to take this rage I'd been holding onto my entire life out on someone in a way punches couldn't suffice.

The Commanding Officer called over the 1MC radio system onboard the ship, "Shipmates, we are in a time of war. Our great country is under attack. We have trained and prepared for this moment our entire careers, but this crew specifically put in tremendous effort as the Navy's 911 carrier. We will be the first on station and leave in 48 hours. Please return to your loved ones, make sure your affairs are in order, and pack up your stuff. We don't know when we'll be returning home."

I felt like I was letting my entire team down. They needed me and I needed them. This was my duty and there is honor in fulfilling duty to your country. On the other hand, the husband in me was relieved because I knew Stephanie was sitting in the Navy Lodge afraid and unsure of what was next. All air travel was stopped, she didn't know any of the spouses, and she was living in a hotel room. She was literally on an island with the potential to be left alone for God knows how long. I walked into the Navy Lodge and set down my seabag and the rest of my stuff I'd accumulated.

"Why do you have all of your stuff?" Stephanie asked.

"The ship's medical officer disqualified me from overseas duty. We're going back to the U.S. as soon as I work out details for my next set of orders."

She was overjoyed and jumped into the air. She tried to be considerate of how I felt because she knew I was devastated. I wouldn't be able to defend freedom with my brothers and sisters in war, but, after spending eight months by herself, she also knew she wouldn't have to be alone again. The following week, we received orders to San Diego and transferred to another command.

———

San Diego was paradise. We loved every second of it. We spent time making friends and lived across the street from where my favorite NFL team, the Los Angeles Chargers, played. The palm trees, beach, and nightlife were everything we wanted. We took full advantage of it all. After a tumultuous first six years in the Navy, we settled in because we knew my orders would keep us there for three years.

I went to college at night to get my degree with the expectation that I would leave the Navy once my contract was finished. Our life was about to take a huge leap forward during this tour and I was about to have another piece of my dream family.

About two years after we got to San Diego, Stephanie came out of the bathroom and told me her period was late. She'd just gotten off of birth control 2 months earlier so I knew she might be pregnant.

The biggest smile of my life spread across my face. "Do you think you're pregnant already?" I bounced up and down like a kid in a candy store waiting for her response.

"I'm not really sure, but it's possible. Let's grab a couple of pregnancy tests to check."

I couldn't drive to CVS fast enough. I wanted her to take them in the store bathroom right away. I was so excited. I knew she wouldn't. I'd have to wait until we got home, but I couldn't help talking about how amazing we'd be as parents.

Stephanie walked out of the bathroom after taking a couple of tests. The sparkle in her eye told me that she had great news. "We're going to be parents. I took three tests and they all came back positive."

"Yes! I'm so happy right now!"

I couldn't believe it; we were officially going to be parents. The dreams I'd had as a kid were coming true! I gave her a huge hug. I couldn't sit still, I was so excited. I needed to tell everyone, so I called Aunt Dianna, Faith, and Grandma to tell them all that we were going to have a baby.

I knew this was my chance to change my legacy forever and give my baby the life I never had.

CHAPTER 17
THE MIRACLE OF LIFE

Nine months seems like an eternity when you're anxiously waiting for your child to be born. Reflecting back, the time goes so fast, and I needed it to grow before my daughter was born. My emotions during those months were pretty intense. I experienced some hesitancy and fear. I didn't want to replicate the abuse I'd experienced to my daughter. I knew I wouldn't hit her, but I didn't want my anger to come through or manifest itself in other ways. I'd seen Dad and Gail's tension grow when they had Patrick and how their relationship spiraled. I didn't want the same thing to happen for me and Stephanie.

On the other side of the fear was resolution. I knew my children would never experience the horrid abuse I'd been through, and I knew it was my responsibility to make 100% sure of it. I had control over their lives and protection, and felt it was my most important responsibility in life to ensure they grew up in a healthy home. I wanted to give them the start in life I never had.

I thought the more privileged of a start I gave them, the further away my lineage would be from ever going back to the torture I'd endured.

Stephanie looked at me as we drove through the KFC drive thru. "I think my water might have broken. I'm not sure except that things feel a bit different."

My heart leapt! It was time. Time to welcome my daughter into the world. Time to take our little family to the next level. We raced home and called the midwife at the hospital. She told us to wait a couple of hours to be positive that Stephanie's water truly broke and to wait until contractions got closer together.

We knew it was going to be a long night, so we laid in our bed and relaxed while Stephanie's body got ready. I dozed off and dreamt about my firstborn daughter, playing her life in my mind. Stephanie woke me up from my short nap and told me it was time to go. I grabbed our go bag, the car seat, clothes, diaper bag, and anything else our Lamaze class told us we needed to be successful day one parents. I ran to the garage and pulled the Toyota 4Runner around to the front of the apartment. She jumped in and off we went.

I sang one of my silly songs to break the tension. "Here we go. We're about to get our baby. This time it's for real. There's definitely no maybe."

I could tell by Stephanie's laugh that it broke the nervous feeling of the upcoming labor. I was thankful that I could still make her smile even during these situations.

The next twelve hours were intense. Stephanie's body struggled to push the baby out, even with Pitocin. I started to get worried; she looked like she'd run a marathon and was exhausted. But she continued to push with each contraction, showing me a strength I'd never seen from her. Finally, with a last push, Monica entered the world.

A flood of emotion ran over me. A hot wave filled my entire body in one moment; the magic and awe creating a euphoria unlike anything I ever felt. I cried and felt the happiest I'd ever felt in my life. The love for Monica was stronger than anything I ever thought possible. Monica was breathtaking and the most beautiful thing I'd ever seen. I cut her umbilical cord and watched as the nurses cleaned her off and placed her back on Stephanie's chest. Her tiny hands and feet fit in the palm of my hand. Her half-opened almond-shaped eyes made me fall in love instantly.

My heart was so full I felt like it could burst open. I looked back and forth between my wife and newborn daughter. I could see happy memories playing inside the window to my soul. Happy visions of our life flashed through my head.

This is exactly what I'd always dreamed of. I'm so lucky and blessed to have these two amazing humans in my life. Thank you, God, for answering my prayers.

I prayed to God. "Please give me the strength and wisdom to guide and protect my family for all time. Please don't let them ever experience the things I did.

Help me love them unconditionally, protect them fully, and help me be an amazing father."

Exhausted, we all fell asleep. The intimate feeling of having Monica on Stephanie's chest and my hands over them both gave me the most peace I'd ever had in my 27 years on earth.

———

Eight months later, our tour in San Diego finished. Our next adventure took us to Jacksonville, Florida where I'd finish out my Naval commitment. We closed on our first home just before we moved. I was proud of our house and knew we'd make it perfect for our family. I had an internal fire to create a different legacy for my family and worked every day to be the best at whatever was put in front of me. Monica added rocket fuel to the fire and made it a raging inferno to get as far away from my past as possible so she would never experience a second of what I did.

I arrived at my new command and was told on the first day that I'd been promoted to E-6. I was excited! This meant more responsibility, more money, and better opportunities. I needed to secure a great career and finish my degree to be absolutely sure I could provide for my family the way I felt they deserved.

After a couple of weeks, my new boss, Jesús, sat me down and asked me what I wanted to accomplish while I was at the command. He told me about moving as a kid from Venezuela to the U.S. He started in the Navy enlisted and was now a Lieutenant Commander. Jesús had a swagger and confidence I gravitated to. He was very successful, and I wanted to be successful, too, so I was ready to learn from him.

Jesús became my second life-changing male mentor. His friendship changed the course of my life. I told Jesús my goals at the command were to finish my degree, try again for an officer program, and be Sailor of the Year. He didn't even flinch and looked at me for a full minute to see if my confidence wavered. I waited for him to respond.

"OK, I respect your goals and I've done it myself. I will do everything in my power to make it happen, but you're going to work your ass off for it. I mean really earn it."

I was all in! Someone who believed in me and would help me forge a path to success was what I needed. It was quite a few years since I'd had a mentor like Corey, and it was everything. I appreciated Jesús for investing into me.

"Say no more. I want to earn it and am not afraid of hard work. Just guide me along the way and I'll do whatever is necessary"

Over the next year, Jesús put me in positions to succeed far beyond my paygrade. He embedded me in projects normally reserved only for officers, then stepped aside to start new ones, leaving me responsible and typically one of the only people who understood what was going on.

I became the top-ranked sailor at the command, earned Sailor of the Year honors, finished my degree, and applied for Officer Candidate School (OCS). A glowing endorsement from the Admiral made my application incredibly competitive. Now it was a waiting game to get the results. If I was accepted, I would leave for OCS in a couple months. If I wasn't accepted, I had my degree and would become a civilian a little over a year later. It was a win-win.

Two months later, the Admiral called me to his office. I was used to joining him to cover intelligence reports, but this wasn't the normal time. I walked into his office. Jesús and some of the other senior officers were waiting for me.

"Well, IS1 McKinley, we got your officer package back today. The selection process was really tough. From what I was told, only one person was selected out of almost 200 applicants," the Admiral said.

He had a stone-cold poker face. *Man, I cannot take another disappointment in the Navy. If this doesn't happen for me then I'm going to have to really move into the civilian world.*

Then they all started laughing. "Congratulations, you are the one person! You did it. We're all really proud of you and wanted to welcome you into the officer ranks together. Amazing job, son. You're going to make one hell of an officer. We're happy to have you join the wardroom."

I jumped up, yelling out, "Hell yes! Thank you all for your support and for helping me submit such a strong application. No doubt your endorsements had an impact on my selection."

I felt elated and relieved all at once. I couldn't believe it. I was going to actually be a Naval Officer. The goal I had in the office with the Naval Recruiter ten years earlier was finally happening. After being disqualified from submarines, the Enlisted Commissioning Program, and overseas duty, I finally broke through. I finally did it! I wasn't ever going to stop striving for more. I learned to never give up on my goals.

Earning a commission was the reason I stayed in the Navy for ten more years and retired. But there were a few more milestones and hurdles to overcome.

———

I arrived at the Officer Candidate School parking lot in Pensacola, Florida at 0700 hours, fully ready for three months of training focused on militarizing and preparing all of us for the responsibility of being a Naval Officer. Officer candidates from all walks of life arrived at the parking lot around the same time. We all got to know each other while we waited.

Most of them seemed nervous and appeared to be new college graduates who thought training was going to be like "Full Metal Jacket." Two of the forty of us had ten years of experience in the Navy, so we decided to take charge and gather everyone together.

The blacktop was hot and the humid muggy Florida air stuck to you like a giant heating pad. We'd waited about an hour for someone to come get us. I was getting restless until a white van sped through the parking lot towards the group, sliding to a halt about ten feet from us.

Three candidate officers jumped out and started screaming at us, attempting to shock and awe the new class. I'd been through boot camp before, so it was comical when some of the new candidates looked like they were going to run back to their cars and leave. I knew this was only the beginning and the real training would start on Wednesday when the Marine Corps drill instructors took over.

"Wake Up Wednesday" was the first real evolution of the training. Marines are a rare breed and these drill instructors wanted to mentally break at least one of the officer candidates on the first day. It was like a badge of honor for them and something necessary to remove anyone not fully committed.

SLAM!! The double doors of the barracks smashed open, creating a shocking effect that reverberated through everyone not used to mental and physical confrontation. I spent my whole life getting yelled at, berated, and tested. Plus, I understood what they were doing, so the DI's intimidation tactics didn't faze me very much.

The barracks was wide open with thirty bunk beds against the walls and an open space in the middle big enough for people to walk around and do physical training. Twelve Marine Corps drill instructors came in yelling and hollering orders, barking so loud it made it difficult to understand what they were saying. They slammed trash cans together and threw them across the room, almost hitting us. I was a bit shocked by the intensity but could see real fear in the faces of the other candidates.

We all stood at attention with our toes on the line. Some people received help in the form of a quick shake or push from the drill instructors.

One of the DI's yelled out, "So, all of you want to be Naval Officers because you couldn't handle being in the Marines. I think you guys are scared. Because of that, we're not leaving until someone quits. Grab your seabags and start running!"

We all grabbed our seabags and began to run single file around a large circle. We only stopped when instructed to start eight-count body builders, squats, push-ups, or any other exercises they ordered us to do.

I whispered to the person in front of me who kept dropping their full seabag, "Keep going. They are trying to break you. Be mentally stronger; It will only last for so long. You got this." Another candidate dropped his sea bag and started crying thirty minutes into the beat down. All twelve of the DI's started yelling in his face, telling him to quit.

"You're weak, soft, and not ready for this life. Not ready for combat. Not ready to put your life on the line for your brothers and sisters. Just quit and give everyone else a break so we can go about our day."

His voice trembled and the look of defeat was evident as he stared at the ground. I heard him mumble that he quit, which was immediately followed by laughs from the DI's. Their laughter sounded like a pack of hyenas. They all cheered as they found their first victim of the day.

Our class DI said, "Anyone who thought this was a game and easy better just quit with him. If you don't have the intestinal fortitude to push yourself to the limit here then you're going to get someone killed in combat. Anyone else?!"

We endured six more hours of exercise. At thirty years old, it was more difficult than before but there was no way I would even consider quitting. I called on years of pain, anger, and isolation that fueled my mission to change my legacy. I knew this was a monumental piece in doing so. Stephanie, Monica, and our unborn daughter, Brianna, gave me purpose to run through anything.

The next three months raced by. It was finally graduation week. Unlike my enlisted bootcamp graduation, I had a lot of my family fly in to see the

290 | MONSTERS IN MY HOUSE

ceremony and support such a big milestone. I was excited to see everyone and thankful they were coming. Graduation week was amazing, I picked Stephanie and Monica up from the airport, and after 3 months of not seeing them, I couldn't wait until I gave them hugs and kisses.

Stephanie looked beautiful. She was eight months pregnant and glowing. I was overjoyed to see that our daughter, Brianna, was almost ready to join us and ecstatic I would be able to be there for the rest of Stephanie's pregnancy. Monica was the cutest and ran through the airport when she saw me. She yelled out "Daddy!" and sprinted towards me, pulling her Dora the Explorer backpack that matched her shirt to give me a hug. I felt blessed to have such an amazing family and people who completed the essence of my being.

Graduation day was here. I slid on my cleanly pressed Navy choker white uniform and attached the ribbons, medals, warfare pins, and rank insignia. I took time to make sure it was pinned on with precision. I shined my white shoes one last time the night before, and the black brim of my cover reflected in the sun as I got ready to go join the formation of other graduates. Stephanie was beaming.

"I'm so proud of you and appreciative of how hard you work for our family."

I puffed out my chest and walked a little taller knowing I had the personal and professional success I'd been striving for my whole life.

We walked to the car, and I heard the "ooh" and "ahh" from my family as they saw me in my officer uniform for the first time. I dropped all of them off at the parade grounds and drove back to get in formation with my training class. We marched towards the parade field for pass and review, an integral part of becoming an officer (and an amazing show for families). I thought to myself about how far I'd come.

I remembered the suffering I'd been through in what seemed like ten lifetimes ago and I started getting choked up. I looked up at the sky, thanking God for protecting me in my darkest hours and providing me with the life I'd always dreamt of. It was an emotional and humbling moment between God and me.

We hit the parade field and I refocused my energy. I was emotional inside but kept full military bearing during the ceremony. I looked straight ahead, resisting the temptation to look into the stands for my family. The weeks of practice made the precision of the march crisp, each person's hands a quarter of an inch from their pants seam, fists closed and lightly rubbing against our uniform with every swing of our arms. Each officer was heel-to-toe in lockstep with our DI.

"Eyes, right." Everyone's focus turned to their families seated in front of us as we marched past them.

A tear ran down my cheek as I made eye contact with Stephanie, Monica, Aunt Dianna, Faith, and the rest of my family. They looked so happy, waving and supporting me every step of the way.

"Eyes, front." The entire class snapped their heads forward.

"Mark time, march." We all marched in place.

"Ready, halt." Each officer took a left then right step before coming to a complete stop.

The Master of Ceremonies took the families through the journey of the last twelve weeks before announcing we were officially graduated. We all threw our covers into the air and hugged each other in elation. We forged a bond by taking a rag tag set of individuals and created a formidable fighting force. The last part of the ceremony was the first salute. My uncle is a second-generation retired sailor after my grandfather so it felt tremendous to have him there in his dress uniform to give me my first salute. It was like he handed off the legacy of service to our country to a new generation— to me!

Stephanie, Monica, and I returned to Stephanie's parents in North Carolina where she stayed while I was in training. The Navy allowed me to work with the officer recruiter during this time as it was only two weeks until Stephanie's delivery date. The Navy allowed me three months to get my family situated and purchase a home back in Virginia Beach, where we'd be stationed. I was appreciative that I could focus solely on my growing family. Once I was done with Intelligence Officer School, I would be on deployment for months at a time.

———

The day came for Brianna to be born. Stephanie told me her contractions were getting close and we prepared to drive to the hospital. We knew exactly what we were doing this time, so it was less stressful. I'd shown myself I was a great and loving father, so I didn't have any of the same fears as I did before Monica was born. Instead, I was over the moon with excitement. Brianna completed our family.

We jumped in the car and left when the contractions were about twenty minutes apart. I drove with care and speedy precision as we navigated the back country roads and headed towards Charlotte. We got into the hospital just as her contractions got closer and were placed in a beautiful delivery room that looked more like a hotel. The room had a soaking tub, tile floors, a private bathroom, and all of the medical devices slid into the wall. It was serene and relaxing.

Stephanie and I talked about the elation of adding another daughter to our family and dreamt about how great of a big sister Monica would be. Brianna joined our family at 5 the next morning. The same emotions I'd felt when Monica was born flooded my body as I witnessed the miracle of life for a second time. Brianna's beautiful eyes looked right at me like she already knew I was her daddy. Her tiny hands, feet, and head fit perfectly on Stephanie's chest as we all peacefully bonded. I knew her life was full of potential and promise. I made the same commitment of always doing my best to protect her and give her the best life.

My little family and my boyhood dream was completed that night in Charlotte.

———

The next couple of years were a whirlwind as I completed Intelligence Officer School and left for a deployment on the USS Enterprise to the Arabian Sea. Military service is a sacrifice and, although I desperately never wanted to miss a major milestone, I missed Brianna's first steps and first birthday. I knew all four of us would make sacrifices for the next several years until I could retire from the Navy, but I needed to balance family and military life if I was going to change my legacy.

I took the legacy of leadership Corey and Jesús passed down to me wherever I went. They both had an immense impact on my life and helped me be a better man and professional. I wanted to have the same impact on the sailors I was leading. I knew a heartfelt approach was how I was called to lead. I had lofty expectations of others and myself but knew my leadership style would provide the type of culture I wanted while building team-first winning organizations.

Brianna and Monica grew bigger by the day. I enjoyed every second of being a father. Well, maybe I didn't enjoy some of the crying nights when they were babies, but everything else was a joy. I played with them, and we made up games like, crash, ricochet, run, horsey rides, and a few others where they'd run into me or I'd throw them towards our couch that had huge cushions.

We'd all go to the park and swing, eat dinner at the table every night together, and pray that the Lord continue to bless our family and those in need. I loved acting goofy and fun with them and never cared what anyone else thought. Stephanie was the perfect partner and, even when we'd have normal marital struggles, we always had each other's back. The kids' giggles, laughs, and love healed the deepest recesses of my heart and soul—the parts where I didn't think I would ever be whole again. I still had some work to do in finding forgiveness, but I was the happiest I'd ever been in my life.

During the next few years, I met a sailor who trusted me enough to share her abusive story with me. She was angry, confused, and in despair from years of abuse, all feelings I knew well and had worked through myself. The interactions we had changed my life forever and gave me a different perspective on how my abusive past could positively affect others. The renewed perspective I found healed the pain I held onto in the darkest, locked, and secret rooms of my soul. I will be forever grateful to her for trusting me.

Fourteen years into my career, I had the opportunity to be a Division Officer for almost 200. I loved joking with them and used levity as a way to connect with all of them and keep a family atmosphere. The synergy was palpable, and we had each other's backs no matter what. We worked hard and played hard, operating at extremely high levels and expecting the best effort from everyone. My desk was just outside "the pit," where all of the enlisted sailors sat. I was close enough to be ready to support when they needed me, but far enough to give them space to accomplish their mission.

I could tell one of the sailors was having an off day as she walked past me one morning. It wasn't like her to not say something when she walked past. Because of the camaraderie we built, she was always quick to say a joke or fire back at me.

After her third pass, I called out, "Dang, you're not even going to say 'Good morning?'" A smile crested my lips.

"It's just not a good day, I've been going through some serious personal things and I feel lost."

I sensed the state of despair she was in, something I knew all too well from years of dealing with my abuse.

I hate seeing anyone in pain, so I stood up and asked her to take a walk with me, hoping I could reach her somehow. We opened the heavy steel soundproof door separating the secure intelligence area to the rest of the building and walked through the halls of the command.

I asked her what was bothering her and if I could help. I felt that she wanted to talk about it but was hesitant and protective of her emotions. I opened up to her about some of the abuse I struggled with in my past, and how it left me as a half empty and angry person for a long time. I talked with her about how I worked through the pain to unlock another level of myself.

She breathed a sigh and, with tears in her eyes, started to share with me. She told me she had some things happen to her as a kid and that she was struggling with it as an adult. I could tell sharing some of my story set her mind at ease and she felt safer talking to me about what happened to her.

She told me about severe trauma and abuse that happened between when she was six to sixteen years old and, as a new mom, she couldn't comprehend how her mother could be so despondent and in denial. I could feel her holding back the flood of emotions sitting just inside her chest and trying to be courageous as possible. My heart hurt for her, and I could feel every part of her pain.

Remembering exactly how I felt at her age, I wished I could take away the hurt and replace it with joy. She cried and I listened for over an hour as she poured her heart out to me. Her pain was being released and her soul was cleansed with every word she spoke. I told her I thought she was a warrior for being able to live through her childhood and how proud I was that she wanted to break the generational cycle.

As we talked some more, I asked her if she would be OK with me trying to get her some therapy through the command. No one would know about it, and she could see the therapist during working hours so that she could get her daughter from daycare in the afternoon. I told her I would take care of any concerns and she would only need to tell them Lieutenant McKinley knew about her appointments.

She agreed and started seeing the therapist while still at command. I saw the profound change in her during these sessions. A true joy started taking hold and an unshakeable confidence grew in her.

Halfway through her therapy, she was transferred to a local ship. We talked about the importance of continuing her sessions. She assured me she would continue the healing journey until she conquered her pain and made sure her daughter wouldn't be negatively affected by it. She thanked me for my help and told me she was excited that the best was yet to come. We said our goodbyes. I expected to never hear from her again and wished her the best of luck.

I looked up six months later to see her standing in front of me.

I was caught a little off guard. "You're not going to say anything when I'm standing at your desk?" she joked.

She asked if I had time to take a walk with her as she wanted to update me about her new job on the ship and fill me in on the rest of the therapy sessions. She had a glow and swagger about her that I'd never seen. I couldn't help but smile knowing she'd done the work to heal. We sat down at a picnic bench just outside the back door and she took me through the last six months. She said her journey was painful and at times she wanted to run, but today she felt powerful and like a new person ready to conquer the world.

Towards the end of our conversation, she paused and I saw her eyes fill with tears.

"I want you to know how close I was to taking my life when you intervened. I've always felt that people didn't care, and you showed me compassion I never received during my childhood. You are the first man I've ever met who didn't want something in return for the help you gave. I will never forget you. You saved my life and I wanted to come back to tell you personally the impact you've made on me. You talked about speaking your truth being a key to overcome the shame of the secrets I was holding. You were right, and the more I speak about my trauma, the happier I feel. I feel more empowered and confident that my past won't hold me back ever again."

I like to think that I typically know the right thing to say, but on this day I didn't have any words. This wasn't a compliment; it was the most humbling thing a human being ever said to me. I was speechless, stopped in my tracks in a moment that changed me forever. I realized for the first time that by sharing my own story I could also help people overcome their abuse and get their power back.

I gave her a hug. "Thank you for trusting me with your most inner secrets and I genuinely appreciate you letting me be a small part of your journey. I don't take what you said lightly and appreciate you letting me know that I made an impact on you more than you can ever imagine. I'm so proud of you and excited for your future."

We said our goodbyes and she's continued to live a joyful and abundant life.

My life changed forever since the day we spoke. That conversation prepared me for the next season of my life. I knew I would share my story with anyone who was struggling with their past, to create a safe space, and guide them on their healing journey. By giving the abused their power back, they could speak their truth and break the generational cycle of trauma that permeates so many families.

I continued my Naval career until I retired after twenty years. I'm proud of my Navy heritage and blessed to have met incredible mentors who played a huge part in taking my life to the next level. I have many shipmates I still call friends today. I hope my legacy of giving back, and mentoring the next generation of sailors, is carried on through those who were willing to be mentored by a man who really cared about them as people.

After retiring, I took a chance on trying something totally new and challenged myself in corporate America. The path was successful. I was promoted three times in five years and ended my career as an executive for a Fortune 300 company. I loved the challenge of creating team-first organizations with a family atmosphere. I excelled at teaching leaders that it's OK to be a heart-centered champion for your people and, by doing so, you can create record company performance. It was transformational. Most companies only focus on key performance indicators and metrics to determine performance. By putting the team first, my groups and the incredibly talented people I worked with achieved record results, smashing company performance. The best part was that I took care of people first and built real relationships. I still talk to many of them today.

I'm blessed beyond belief to be married to Stephanie twenty-two years and together for twenty-five. She has loved and supported me while we grew into the life partners and humans we are today. She is my light, my joy, and, most of all, my soulmate. God gifted her to me at a time in my life when I was at a fork in the road. Her unshakable faith and unwavering patience made me a better man and I'm grateful we get to experience life together. This memoir is a testament to her love. She knew my story needed to be told and encouraged me to leave corporate America to write it.

Monica and Brianna are two of the most extraordinary young women I've ever known. They are compassionate, hardworking, empathetic, and loving. They make me proud and I have no doubt they will continue to elevate our family legacy in their own way. Wanting to be the best father and example of a man I could for them motivated me in my darkest hours and biggest setbacks. Being their dad completed me and healed my soul in a way that is nothing short of miraculous. Monica and Brianna completed my humanity, and I will be forever grateful I get to be their dad.

CHAPTER 18
KEYS TO LIVING AN EXTRAORDINARY LIFE

"Your history does not define your destiny" is my favorite quote by TD Jakes.

I live my life by this mantra. I spent years broken, beaten, ashamed, terrified, and, ultimately, shattered into a million pieces. But the spirit is strong and powerful. Everything meant to break me only made me unstoppable. I wasn't able to unlock the gifts from my trauma until I did the work to heal. Once I did, I found amazing levels of grit, empathy, resilience, compassion, and a powerful mindset only Warriors, like us, can understand.

For many people, it's easier to stay a victim and in comfortable pain. I know because I did it for years. Fear of the unknown stopped me from taking uncomfortable action and moving forward. But you have to know that on the other side of fear is victory. There is a light shining in the darkness ready to show you the way out. There is an abundance of joy, love, happiness, success, and everything else you deserve waiting for you to make the decision to run into the unknown and into the light! It doesn't matter where you started in life, what kind of cards you were dealt, or even your age, you have the power to change your legacy. And it starts today!

Too many people tell those who've been through trauma to "Get over it" or they ask "Why can't you move on?" Oftentimes, we don't know where to even start. This memoir is meant to inspire healing. I want to share with you the tangible steps I used, and teach others, on how I overcame my tortuous abuse and thrived *because* of it.

Step 1: Speak Your Truth

So many of us never have an opportunity to speak our truth because of our own self-doubts or the fear of what people will think or the fear of causing a family rift or even being silenced purposefully by others around us. The first, and sometimes toughest, step in our healing journey is speaking our truth out loud to at least one person.

Doing so allows you to take the pain sitting just inside your chest and release it from your being. It allows the shame of the secrets you've locked away for so long, poisoning your soul, an antidote unlike any other. Once you share with one trusted person, it's no longer a secret and you can put down the heavy pack you've been holding onto. Find a friend, coach, therapist, family member, or someone who will listen. Trust me, you have someone. And if you don't feel like you do, **then find me**. I'll listen so you can speak your truth. The pain you're hanging onto has no place in your heart any longer!

Speaking my truth came in phases, both verbally and spiritually. I didn't just wake up one day and let everything out at once. It started with a drip until I was comfortable enough to let everything I kept hidden from the light flow out of me. I told myself I was fine and I'd moved on but the truth was that I had a lot of pent up aggression, pain, shame, and other emotions I needed to resolve. No amount of fighting, weights, or basketball would release the poison crushing me from the inside out. I had to find a different release. Speaking my truth quickly showed itself as a path I needed to walk down and was the antidote for my broken soul.

I started sharing what I could with Aunt Dianna when I moved in with her just before my sixteenth birthday. My truth, and the emotion connected to it, came out little by little. I suffered in silence outside of those conversations and didn't share anything but an extremely watered down version of my reality with anyone else in my teens. Even my closest friends didn't realize the torture I'd endured.

I found that each time I shared my truth it became easier to let the emotion tearing my soul apart go with each word I spoke. Each time I shared, another piece of my story would surface, and another piece of shame was knocked from my heart.

Once I met Stephanie and our relationship became more serious, I told her the rest of my truth. I'd spoken for the first time about events I'd kept locked away in the deepest parts of my soul. It was like rocket fuel in my healing journey. Over time, speaking my truth accelerated and became more purposeful, especially after I helped the young sailor start sharing her truth for the first time and she told me it saved her life. Once I realized the impact my truth had on her, I knew I had to share my story with others in pain so they felt safe to do the same.

Step 2: Acceptance and Acknowledgment

Once you've spoken your truth, you have to accept your abuse for what it is and move forward. This isn't a time to sugarcoat or dismiss your reality. We cannot change what happened to us, but we can change today and tomorrow by leveling up through the healing process. Once you've accepted the reality of what happened to you, allow yourself to feel the emotions connected to it. I spent time crying, screaming, being angry, mourning my childhood, and every other range of emotion you can think of and have probably felt yourself. Accept the trauma, feel the emotion, release the pain, and keep moving forward.

I always accepted the abuse and reality of its intensity for what it was, but I struggled with accepting the emotions tied to the abuse. It was easier for me to say what happened without acknowledging the pain I still felt inside. I kept a tough exterior and never cried, because I felt like showing emotion made me look weak. I felt like I'd spent an entire childhood crying and the scared little boy inside of me was afraid it wouldn't stop if I ever let the emotion go.

I tried to focus on the future by keeping myself busy with marriage, fatherhood, friends, and my career. I resolved myself to only look forward because the present and future were the only things I could control. But I also found that you can't run from pain. At some point, you have to face the pain and replace it with power and happiness. To do so, it requires you to acknowledge the real and raw emotions connected to your trauma.

The first time I ever acknowledged how I felt was when I was nineteen and at church. I cried for a long time after asking God for help. I didn't know what I was even asking for in the moment, I just knew my soul was stirred in a way I'd never felt previously. The pain poured out of me like a waterfall cascading over the rocks with a thunderous roar. When I let the emotion go, it was like coming up for air after almost drowning.

The moment didn't fully resolve my pain but was a huge jumpstart in my emotional and spiritual awakening. The amazing, uplifting, cleansing feeling I had when I was done crying showed me how important dealing with pent up emotions really is. Learning how to let the hurt out, while trusting God enough to give my pain to him, gave me an outlet I was previously unaware of.

Step 3: Forgiveness

Whew, this one was hard for me! There were times I felt like I forgave but something would knock me back into the reality that I didn't. What finally helped me was figuring out that forgiveness was for _me_!

Read the last sentence again before moving on!

Forgiveness isn't about letting your abusers off the hook or telling them that what they did was OK. Forgiveness is about us letting go of the emotion connected to our abuse so we can live a healthy and joyful life. I realized the reason abuse is generational, and perpetrated by family members 78% of the time, is because nobody deals with the pain abuse causes. Families sweep it under the rug to protect their family name or they find that it's too uncomfortable to talk about.

Once I realized hurt people hurt others, and all my abusers were themselves abused, it gave me a better understanding on why it happened to me. It didn't mean I thought it was OK, it just meant I understood, and once I understood, I was able to forgive much easier.

My parents were two broken people who never resolved their childhood trauma and instead continued the generational cycle of abuse on each other and their kids. They didn't have the capacity to love or fight for themselves, much less me and my siblings. The pain they held onto ravaged their happiness and stunted their growth as human beings, allowing them to be only a fraction of what was possible. They drank and did drugs to mask the pain, because it was easier for them to become numb rather than push through the emotions to heal. Their fear of not finding happiness was more powerful than the elation and belief that they could find it. I know firsthand that it's possible and never too late. I pray your belief is your motivator.

As an adult, and after a lot of growth, healing, self-reflection, and wisdom, I reconciled with my father and mother, ultimately finding it in my heart to forgive them. I knew the pain and anger I held onto wasn't doing anything but hurting me and my blossoming family. I knew I didn't want my trauma to limit my potential like I'd seen it do for my parents and instead used my trauma as a driving force for good. Being their son wasn't easy. I've felt frustrated, hurt, disappointed, and sometimes exhausted on too many occasions to count, but forgiving them gave me the personal peace that I wouldn't have found otherwise.

The hardest person to forgive was my stepfather, Bruce. I saw him when I was nineteen and wanted to literally tear his head off (I would have likely done so if he wasn't talking to my sister, Nicole). I don't even think he realized in the moment what I was thinking, but my rage was unlike anything I've felt since. When Nicole got married ten years later, I'd done a lot of work on forgiveness with my parents, but not with Bruce.

I knew leading up to her wedding that I needed to dig in emotionally so I wouldn't ruin her special day. I thought to myself, nobody is born wanting to hurt someone else. What happened to him was so terrible that he uncontrollably beat, belittled, locked me in the basement, and abused me. Instead of still feeling angry, I started to feel sad for the little boy inside of him. I found myself praying for an extremely broken human being and I let go of my hatred.

The night of the wedding, I was able to shake Bruce's hand and tell him congratulations on Nicole's marriage. I was still a bit surprised in the moment. I didn't have malice in my heart for him, and it proved to me that I'd finally found a way to forgive him and move forward with my life. He never knew I forgave him, and we didn't sit by each other and exchange conversation over dinner. I showed myself that night I didn't have anything left to resolve, and the pain he caused me only made me stronger.

Forgiveness is one of the most powerful tools in your healing toolbox. Finding the space in your spirit to really forgive can set your soul free like nothing else can.

Step 4: Exposing Your Superpowers

During the healing journey, you'll find amazing gifts inside your soul previously masked by your pain. Every single person I know who's been through trauma, and healed from it, is the most grit filled, determined, compassionate, empathetic, driven individual I've ever met. The trauma gifts you superpowers, and it's something only healed Warriors like us will understand. When your pain becomes your purpose and you start looking out the windshield of life instead of the rear-view mirror, the impact to your legacy is profound.

My superpowers were unlocked over decades of purposeful and intentional action by working through the first three steps (several times). When I started taking my power back, I focused on uncovering an elevated version of myself. I can say, without a shadow of a doubt, I wouldn't be able to speak at conferences, schools, and events, write this memoir, or have family and career success without the abuse I endured. As my perspective changed from being a victim to being a victor, I've become thankful for the trauma and abuse I endured because it has made me unstoppable.

Once I realized everything in life became about how I mentally handled it, and the only thing I could truly control were my reactions, I started seeing everything in a new light. I now see setbacks and disappointments as opportunities to grow stronger, master a skill, or learn something about myself I haven't considered yet. When you mentally make the decision to see life as happening *for* you and not *to* you, the way you see everything around you starts to change. Your success, momentum, relationships, self-worth, happiness, and ultimately, life's abundance starts finding you!

Once you get to this stage of your journey it's like someone gives you a golden key to a magic box full of treasure, greatness, and the best version of self.

I want to leave you with a few final thoughts:

You are not a victim or survivor, and you are not alone.

Those things meant to knock you down only prepared you for the comeback of your life.

You are still standing. You are still here. You are powerful. And you are a Warrior!

Run headfirst into what scares you the most; fight for yourself and those who deserve all of you.

Time is going to keep passing us by. It already is so why not do the necessary work to unlock your full potential? I can see three, six, twelve months from now when you've made the decision to own your power, own your future, own the new you, a new elevated joyous you who becomes a beacon of light for others still battling like we did.

This is a lifelong journey with ups and downs. It's messy and every day is far from perfect. You will still get triggered, but your ability to handle those situations without spiraling is vastly improved as you heal. Over time, you'll find the downs aren't as drastic and your ups continue to get higher.

Join me, and millions of other Warriors who stand next to you ready to support, cheer, and help you during your journey.

I left corporate America because I felt like my purpose wasn't being fulfilled. God called me to focus on helping people break the generational cycle of abuse and fight to be the hero of their family. God gave me special skills to help those trying to find the light in the darkness a way out.

Like most of you, I've lived through the worst life had to offer. I'm still here standing, fighting, thriving, and living an extraordinary life because of my experiences.

I've been happy for a long time but aligning my vision with God's purpose uncovered another level of joy I didn't even know was missing—a joy I want you to have, too.

The joy of helping you, or anyone else, unlock their superpowers and live a full, happy life is now my mission. This memoir is only the beginning, there is so much more to come!

To be continued…

ACKNOWLEDGEMENTS

Faith – I wouldn't have made it past day one without you trying to protect me along the way. You are the reason I kept my sanity for the first ten years of my life. I'm so appreciative of the relationship we still have today. I love you!

Family and Friends – Thank you for being my supporters, cheerleaders, advocates, and motivation along this amazing ride we call life. You all play a key part in who I am, and where I'm going. I love you all!

Corey – Thank you for having my back since the day we first met. You were the first man I met in the military who believed in me, encouraged me, and helped unlock my full capability. I wouldn't be where I am in life without your mentorship and friendship. Your impact continues to reverberate in the way I conduct myself today. I love you, brother!

Jesús – Thank you for being my biggest champion when I thought I was going to leave the military. Your wisdom, guidance, thoughtfulness, and ability to put me in the right place at the right time catapulted my career and is a primary reason I fulfilled my dream of being a

Naval Officer. Your friendship, mentorship, and guidance continue to impact me today. I love you, brother!

Janine – The Book Publishing Academy and your training is the reason this memoir was done at such a high level. I didn't even know where to start, but your guidance and mentorship helped create something I'm exceptionally proud of. If you want to write a book, find Janine and the Book Publishing Academy. Thank you!

Samantha – Your ability to take what I wrote and edit it into a concise and meaningful memoir was second to none. You are truly a master at your craft. Anyone who needs an editor, contact S'MORLEY'S Editorial Services. I couldn't be more pleased. Thank you!

Ian - JUST WOW! You took an idea I had for the cover and amplified it 1,000 times. I am still in awe of how creative you are. The cover generates emotion, intrigue, and compels a reader to buy the book. You are an extraordinary pro at what you do! Thank you!

ABOUT THE AUTHOR

Walt McKinley is an inspirational speaker, trainer, and author who delivers memorable keynote presentations and training for companies, schools, and events around the world. He speaks on a variety of topics from his extraordinary experiences, including leadership, resilience, positive mindset, and overcoming adversity to help others unlock their full potential using real life experiences.

Walt resides in Arizona with his wife, Stephanie, and two daughters, Monica and Brianna. He is committed to making this world a better place for all of us.

You can book Walt for speaking engagements or training through his website at www.waltmckinley.com

You can also connect with Walt on social media at:

Facebook: www.facebook.com/walter.mckinley.7
Instagram:
www.instagram.com/waltmckinleymotivation/

Made in the USA
Middletown, DE
16 February 2022

61075118R00186